Cinematic Codes Review
Volume III, Issue 2
Summer 2018

Interviews with Scholars

Anna Faktorovich

Anaphora Literary Press

Quanah, Texas

EDITOR-IN-CHIEF

ANNA FAKTOROVICH

EDITORIAL BOARD

NICHOLAS BIRNS • DOUGLAS J. KING
ROBERT HAUPTMAN • WILLIAM IRWIN

ANAPHORA LITERARY PRESS
https://anaphoraliterary.com
director@anaphoraliterary.com
1108 W 3rd Street
Quanah, TX 79252

Book design by Anna Faktorovich, Ph.D.

Copyrights © 2018 by Anna Faktorovich

All rights reserved. No part of this book may be reproduced in any form or by any electronic or mechanical means, including information storage and retrieval systems, without permission in writing from Anna Faktorovich. Writers are welcome to quote brief passages in their critical studies, as American copyrights law dictates.

Printed in the United States of America, United Kingdom and Australia on acid-free paper.

Cover Image: "An Aztec Sculptor" (oil on wood) by George de Forest Brush (1887). Gift (Partial and Promised) of the Ann and Tom Barwick Family Collection: National Gallery of Art.

Published in 2018 by Anaphora Literary Press

Anna Faktorovich—1st edition.

ISSN 2473-3385 (Print)
ISSN 2473-3377 (Online)

Faktorovich, Anna, 1981-, editor.
    Cinematic Codes Review : Volume III, Issue 2 : Interviews with Scholars / Anna Faktorovich
    84 p. ; 9 in.
    ISBN 978-1-68114-477-1 (softcover : alk. paper)
    ISBN 978-1-68114-478-8 (hardcover : alk. paper)
1. Photography—Techniques—Cinematography & Videography.
2. Literary Collections—Interviews.
3. Performing Arts—Film—Guides & Reviews.
PN1-9: Literary Periodicals; PN80-99: Literature Criticism.
801 Philosophy & theory; 805 Serial publications

VOLUME III

ISSUE 2

INTERVIEWS WITH SCHOLARS

―――――――――

ANNA FAKTOROVICH

EDITOR

ANAPHORA LITERARY PRESS
Publisher of fiction, poetry and non-fiction
anaphoraliterary.com

PENNSYLVANIA LITERARY JOURNAL

ISSN#: 2151-3066; 6X9", $15/iss: is a printed journal that runs critical essays, book-reviews, short stories, interviews, photographs, art, and poetry. Also available from EBSCO and ProQuest. One PLJ article won the 2015 CCCC Lavender Rhetoric Award for Excellence in Queer Scholarship. PLJ published *New York Times* bestselling and major award-winning writers such as Larry Niven, Mary Jo Putney, Bob Van Laerhoven and Geraldine Brooks.

DISTRIBUTION:
• In full-text on EBSCO Academic Complete and ProQuest databases.
• On sale as single issues on Amazon, Barnes and Noble.
• YBP/ Coutts distribution
• Annual Subscription: $45: shipping included, 3 issues/ year. No extra fees with electronic or paper checks. 4% for PayPal and 3% for SquareUp.
• Free excerpts of reviews and interviews with best-sellers are publicly available on the Anaphora website.

CINEMATIC CODES REVIEW

**ISSN 2473-3385 (print);
ISSN 2473-3377 (online);
6X9", $15/iss**: features work in all visual genres, especially those with moving pictures, be they music videos, feature films, documentaries, photography, or just about any other mode or genre of art that does not fall into the realm of "literature."

Unsolicited submissions to both journals (scholarship, reviews, interviews) and for Anaphora books are **always warmly welcomed** at director@anaphoraliterary.com, Anna Faktorovich, PhD.

TABLE OF CONTENTS

INTRODUCTION / Anna Faktorovich   6

INTERVIEWS WITH SCHOLARS / Anna Faktorovich

- **Dr. John Milton Hoberman** on Steroids in Policing   7
- **Allen M. Hornblum** on Medical Ethics and Smear Campaigns in Sports   18
- **Professor Michele McArdle Stephens** on Peyote and the Huichol Culture   29

ESSAY

Mixed Reality, the Female Body, and Represented Worlds in Woman on the Edge of Time and Sucker Punch /
Heather Duerre Humann   42

FILM REVIEWS / Samantha Lauer   54

Timelessness and Comfort:
A PHOTOGRAPHY PROJECT / Fabrice Poussin   77

Contributors   *83*

INTRODUCTION

Anna Faktorovich, PhD

This summer issue features three interviews with established researchers and writers. Dr. John Milton Hoberman (University of Texas at Austin) discusses a variety of topics connected with his books, including his most recent book, *Dopers in Uniform*, on steroids in policing. Allen M. Hornblum (covered widely on CBS, CNN, and BBC) replies to questions on medical ethics and smear campaigns in sports, topics related to his latest release, *American Colossus: Big Bill Tilden and the Creation of Modern Tennis*. And professor Michele McArdle Stephens (West Virginia University) touches on the use of the hallucinogenic drug, peyote, in the Huichol culture, the subject of her first major book-length publication, *In the Lands of Fire and Sun: Resistance and Accommodation in the Huichol Sierra, 1723–1930*. Then an essay of film criticism by Heather Duerre Humann (Florida Gulf Coast University) discusses gender in science fiction in the film *Sucker Punch*. Samantha Lauer contributes her regular feature with reviews of recently released films that she particularly enjoyed including *Coco, Mother!* and *Annihilation*. In keeping with CCR's mission to promote all visual and audio arts, the last section is a photography project on the themes of timelessness and comfort from a widely published photographer and author, Fabrice Poussin (Shorter University).

Submissions are always warmly invited; email them with a brief biography to Anna Faktorovich at director@anaphoraliterary.com.

INTERVIEWS WITH SCHOLARS

Interviewer: Anna Faktorovich, PhD

DR. JOHN MILTON HOBERMAN ON STEROIDS IN POLICING

John Milton Hoberman is a Professor of Germanic languages within the Department of Germanic Studies at the University of Texas at Austin. Hoberman has spent thirty years researching, lecturing, and publishing on the various social impacts of anabolic steroids. His books include *Mortal Engines: The Science of Performance and the Dehumanization of Sport* and *Testosterone Dreams: Rejuvenation, Aphrodisia, Doping*. He has published nearly one hundred sports articles and books in American newspapers and magazines and in Der Spiegel. He is fluent in Scandinavian languages as well as German. He is a Fellow of the European committee for sports history.

Dopers in Uniform offers the first assessment of the dimensions and consequences of the felony use of anabolic steroids in major urban police departments. Marshalling an array of evidence, John Hoberman refutes the frequent claim that police steroid use is limited to a few "bad apples," explains how the "Blue Wall of Silence" stymies the collection of data, and introduces readers to the broader marketplace for androgenic drugs. He then turns his attention to the people and organizations at the heart of police culture: the police chiefs who often see scandals involving steroid use as a distraction from dealing with more dramatic forms of misconduct and the police unions that fight against steroid testing by claiming an officer's "right to privacy" is of greater importance. Hoberman's findings clearly demonstrate the crucial need to analyze and expose the police steroid culture for the purpose of formulating a public policy to deal with its dysfunctional effects.

Faktorovich: Your PhD and MA dissertations were in Scandinavian literature (primarily nineteenth century). You have also taught in the Germanic Studies department (Scandinavian and Norwegian) since 1970. In contrast, all of your book publications since 1984 have been in the politics of sports. Some of your contributed chapters have been in Germanic languages. You have written about German sports medicine. And you have done some conference presentations on Scandinavian studies back when you were getting started in the 70s. You started presenting on sports at around that same time as well, and have done many times more presentations in this field. What motivated your research into sport politics? Did you practice sports as a youth? What sports did you play, if so? Do you still play a sport? What do you for exercise? Do you watch a lot of sports or attend games; which ones, if so? Your teaching has been split between Germanic studies and sports studies. Do you prefer teaching sports to a course like "Scandinavian Civilization"? Do you pick your own courses, or are you encouraged to teach primarily in the area in which you received your PhD? Would you advise graduate students to pick an area that they are likely to want to teach for the rest of their lives, or is there a lot of room in academia to publish in a field that is a new interest, and then make a switch into teaching it?

Hoberman: I decided to go into sports studies in January 1971 while in graduate school in Berkeley doing a Ph.D. in Scandinavian Languages and Literature. I had been (and for many years would continue to be) a sub-elite runner who loved the sport. I think the

Black Power demonstrations at the 1968 Mexico City Olympic Games were another stimulus. Being in Berkeley during the period 1966-72 also made me a social critic in a way I had not been before. It dawned on me that the sports world could be analyzed like any other social institution. Today I walk for exercise and watch very little sports on TV or elsewhere. Knowing as much as I do about the way the elite sports world works, it has become impossible for me to be a fan. There are many intellectuals who handle this very differently and are passionate sports fans whose hero worship sometimes makes me wonder about their critical faculties. Someday I will do a book on this topic in as open-minded way as I can manage.

    I have taught a broad range of courses at UT-Austin since 1979, and I have been able to pick almost all my courses. I advise graduate students to do what they know they really want to do, because that is what can sustain you through graduate school and beyond. I also point out that there is good luck and bad luck involved, and that there are no guarantees that these investments will produce satisfying careers. So you have to really believe in the importance of what you choose to do. It's an avocation, like being a good doctor, or a good police officer, or a good priest.

Faktorovich: Why are you particularly interested in hormone testosterone, steroids and other sports related drugs? Have you ever tried steroids? If so, what was your experience like with them? If not, did you have an experience that convinced you that sports-enhancing drugs were a major problem? Where do you draw the line between appropriate enhancements and immoral or inappropriate ones? For example, do you drink coffee, tea, energy drinks or other stimuli, or depressants such as alcohol? If so, why are these socially acceptable, while steroids and other drugs are banned?

Hoberman: Testosterone is a particularly interesting hormone for me (1) because it has been a powerful performance-enhancer that has distorted the performance histories of entire sports, and (2) because it is the "male" hormone, and I am a man. Writing *Testosterone Dreams* was a fine way to learn about my own psychophysiological characteristics. I have never wanted to use supplementary testosterone (the basic anabolic steroid), in part because I am an informed patient who does not trust the advertising put out by pharmaceutical firms and other hormone hustlers. Reading the medical literature on testosterone therapy should make potential patients wary of this exercise in wish-fulfillment. Then talk to doctors who try to get men off their steroid habits. It's a sad story.

"Drawing the line" in a firm and consistent way between appropriate and inappropriate enhancements is essentially impossible. How and why societies either embrace or reject various "drugs" is hugely complicated and involves recognizing the importance of the "social construction" of attitudes and values.

Faktorovich: In one of your best-known books, *Testosterone Dreams*, you talk about your potential "drug-taking coworkers" staying "alert" as "their 'supernormal' stamina may well recalibrate the very idea of normal functioning." The problem, as you see it, is that their spiked "productivity" might mean that "doping" is "compulsory" for all employees to keep up with this extreme level of efficiency. Are you discussing personal experiences you have had with academic coworkers who drink so much coffee that they outperform you? Given the nearly 30-page-long CV that you sent for my review, it seems like you are that one employee in your department who's making everybody else work harder to compete. So, can you clarify your position on this issue?

Hoberman: Regarding the whole issue of what I call "workplace doping," namely "drug-taking co-workers," suffice it to say that these self-medicating coping strategies are very widespread and often go unnoticed or are purposely ignored. I have never encountered a "doped" academic colleague, and I would be dubious about the utility of any such strategy. Many college students have no doubt that Adderall helps them concentrate better on their studies and can help them get into better professional schools. Cocaine on Wall Street for performance-enhancement? I don't know, but it is certainly possible. Besides: what is doping, what is an allowable enhancement, and what is just a "tonic" that is considered a "natural" part of everyday life. These are complicated conceptual problems with few logically satisfying conclusions.

Faktorovich: The Olympics banned caffeine use between 1984 and 2004, limiting intake to under 12 micrograms per milliliter of caffeine, and there has been a debate about bring this ban back into place. Do you think it was a fair ban considering an athlete on an enormous quantity of caffeine might significantly out-perform less caffeinated rivals? Is it more acceptable because it has fewer harmful effects on the body? Why would this make a difference if the bans at the Olympics are supposed to be purely to avoid unfair advantages?

Hoberman: Caffeine has been on and off the banned-substances list. I doubt there is a reliable scientific study that documents, let alone quantifies, the performance-effects of caffeine. It is very hard to prove that a particular biologically active substance improves a specific type of human performance. There is a lot of magical thinking about drugs, including fantasies about pharmacological efficacy that may not accord with reality.

Faktorovich: Your Wikipedia page has a "Controversy" section where you are accused of stirring up racial tensions back in 1997 with *Darwin's Athletes: How Sport Has Damaged Black American and Preserved the Myth of Race*. The author states that anybody looking deeper into the book would be convinced that rather than being racist, you opposed racism. The excerpts quoted discuss how there is still a bias against black athletes despite apparent integration. Another excerpt discusses how the myth of Jackie Robinson's success and other tokenisms have put a blanket of perceived comfort over continuing racism. You have acknowledged that you ventured into a touchy topic as a white man with this book, but you have continued writing about race. So, can you clarify your argument in this book? Are you using statistics to show continued racism? What are the signs that racism is still with us that trouble you? Why wouldn't having a few successful athletes to admire benefit black youths? I have made a similar argument about the overt sexuality and other negative racial stereotypes in Alice Walker's fiction, and how they might have influenced other black arts, and in turn made promiscuity and violence popular, spiking crime among black youth. I tried to avoid making a direct parallel, focusing instead of the facts of the case. I hope your answer can help me to understand my own reaction better as well as your perspective.

Hoberman: *Darwin's Athletes* (1997) was a controversial book, and I am very grateful for that. It was a rough ride for a couple of years, but it enabled me to move beyond the crippling liberal-guilt complex that I am writing about in the current book-in-progress about the Moynihan

Report on the Negro Family (1965). In fact, I was just one of a long series of white authors (think: William Styron and Nat Turner in 1967) who have gotten into trouble for being considered intruders into black space. Was I, to some extent, a naïve white author? Absolutely, though this is almost a tautological statement. Show me a white author on black life who is free of some degree of naïveté. The impact of *Darwin's Athletes* on my life has been so interesting and so complicated that I published a long essay on this topic in 2014 that should be accessible to your readers: "*Darwin's Athletes*: A Retrospective After Fifteen Years."

Faktorovich: *Testosterone Dreams* was reviewed positively in *Playboy* in 2005. I did not know that *Playboy* reviewed scholarly books, but the same page includes short reviews about Freemasonry and China, so apparently, they did. Did you ask your publisher to send a review copy to *Playboy*, send one of your copies, or did tis reviewer find this book by some other way? The review begins thus: "Since testosterone was first synthesized in 1935, it has been hyped as an antidote for old age, sagging libido and girlie-man muscles." Do you think it benefits scholarly books when they can be simplified to the basics, as readers might pick it up assuming that it is approachable? What do you think about the shrinking review sections in most of the major newspapers that have historically published most of the top book reviews? Since you are a tenured professor (and thus probably don't have serious financial motivations), why are you so aggressive in selling your books to the mainstream marketplace? Should other scholars take similar measures? If so, what do you recommend they do to promote themselves as approachable for a general reader?

Hoberman: I can only guess why *Testosterone Dreams* got a short "review" in *Playboy*, but I'm glad it got that additional exposure. I am not concerned about a *Playboy* reader winding up with a book that is more than he may have bargained for, especially since this book, like all of my books, is jargon-free and can be understood by any intelligent person. I'm an anti-elitist author in that sense. As for promotion, I think that an author who has been enabled by a publisher to write a serious book with lots of research and no censorship owes that publisher a maximum effort toward selling as many copies as possible in any reasonable way he can. I've been on radio and TV talking about the book to large audiences, and I'm happy to invest time in this substantial interview to reach a smaller audience. My advice to authors is that they do what they think is appropriate on behalf of their books. Some authors will not care much about audience size. I do, because I always think that the social policy issues in my books should be exposed to as many people as possible.

Faktorovich: I have read some of the other prior reviews you sent to me with interest. Most reviewers from science journals tend to insert some negative criticism alongside positive comments. One that stood us is from *The Journal of Clinical Investigation* on your *Testosterone Dreams* book. The review starts with a few typos of its own: "Hoberman, John; . *Testosterone*… 2005.University of California Press.: Berkeley, USA.390…" The semicolon with a space after it and then a strange period obviously bothers me as ex-English professor. Why isn't there something before the period? Then the lack of spaces after a couple of the periods that follow and the strange period before the colon after the name of the press are also frustrating. Did they bother you too? It's hard to imagine how Cynthia Kuhn managed to create these problems. When my students attempt making automated citations to avoid remembering the formula, they sometimes make similar glitches. I have noticed some misspellings and glitches like this in the mentions I have had in the media. I have always wondered how these guys can be so critical and nitpicky and yet leave major mistakes in their own writing. What are your thoughts on this. Either way, here is the part that drew my attention to this article: "The absence of science limited my enthusiasm for the book. For example, the author is bemused about the failure of testosterone to catch on as a medicine but mainly dismisses the side effects of testosterone and doesn't even consider the differences between the amounts used medically and the suprapharmacologic doses used by athletes." What is your response to this criticism? It particularly affected me because I was prescribed a nasal steroid for my chronic sinuses problem, and I believe using this drug triggered me to gain around a hundred pounds, which I only lost via a vegan diet a year ago after a decade of being obese. I'm pretty sure that using steroids on-and-off for a couple of years contributed to the weight gain, but I definitely don't have any scientific proof of it. I did start exercising regularly in this period as well (for some reason). Did you consider these types of steroid uses as you were researching this book? What do you think about the connection between steroids and weight gain? Would you agree with the reviewer that your book is completely devoid of "science"? Have you considered writing a book in this field with a scientist who might research the scientific end to cancel out these types of doubters; if not, why not? Reviewers frequently tend to criticize what writers leave out of books. Isn't the biggest part of good writing what you leave out? In other words, would a book be infinitely long if a writer does not leave anything that a reviewer might want to read about out?

Hoberman: My response to the "absence of science" commentary is that the reviewer cannot have paid much attention to the book. For example, I was not "bemused" about anything. I attributed the lack of a mass market for testosterone to the sexual conservatism of that era, namely the furor over the Kinsey Reports of 1948 and 1953. The claim that *Testosterone Dreams* is devoid of science is nonsensical. Perhaps the social and medical history of testosterone therapy do not count as science to this reviewer.

I assume the steroids you were using were corticosteroids rather than the sex hormone testosterone, which is the subject of the book.

I do not expect to be writing books with scientists to fend off doubts about the "science" content of my books. The whole point of my science-related books, whether they deal with hormones or medical racism, is to offer the social and political and historical contexts of the science that is being done.

Faktorovich: The topic of police doping has crept into your books and articles many times. *Dopers in Uniform* seems to be your first book-length study solely on this subject. You explain that the motivation for this focus is the rise of the Black Lives Matter movement, which has raised public awareness of the use of deadly force by police officers. Despite the "Blue Wall of Silence", you took a rather scientific approach to this study, gathering statistics on usage. In the chapter about what is publicly known about police steroid use, you give statistics that indicate that most police shooting cases are dismissed, but no clear statistics on the percentage of officers who are using steroids. You mention that one sign of the rate of usage is apparent from the 248 law enforcement officers and firefighters that were proven to be using steroids when Dr. Joseph Colao dropped dead at forty-five after prescribing it to them. Given these statistics, this single doctor was prescribing steroids to around four officers per district. How many officers could there have been in those districts, and how many officers used other doctors? Have you considered other less direct methods of gathering this information despite the lack of systematic testing? How can researchers who are involved in Black Lives Matter discover the rates of steroid usage in their local police departments? Is the data accessible to the general public? Did you have to make any formal requests for this information? Have you looked into what percentage of police-involved shootings involve officers who are using steroids? Are all police officers involved in shootings tested for mind-altering substances, including steroids as part of the investigation? If not, should these findings be made public?

Hoberman: These are all excellent questions, and it is currently impossible to produce satisfactory answers to most of them. Why is this the case? Because police departments are not interested in detecting or publicizing officers' illicit and illegal anabolic steroid use. It is, therefore, impossible to know how many officers are using or how many are getting drugs from unethical doctors. We do not know how many suspicious police shootings are related to steroid use. The secrecy that pervades police departments is currently an insuperable obstacle to gathering various kinds of information. I did not make formal requests for information (1) because I would not have expected to get answers, and (2) because police officials don't produce most of the information one might request. Should they produce information about officer conduct and make it public? Yes, but the political pressure that might bring about such a reform is simply not there. The crisis-plagued Chicago Police Department provides one example of this intransigence.

Faktorovich: You also explain that police unions have prevented standardized testing of police officers for steroid use citing their privacy rights. You clearly don't think that privacy concerns are relevant when it comes to steroid usage during policing. Why not? One telling indicator that American police officers are too doped up is comparing American and UK cop shows. In the UK, the cops are frequently very short, include a lot of female officers, lack muscle definition and are generally very polite in their approach to potential suspects. *Cops* and the like, in contrast, includes very tall men with exploding muscles, dead stares and a very rough attitude that assumes guilt and assumes suspects are going to resist. Naturally, seeing an extremely aggressive and muscular cop approaching might make suspects respond by running away or having a fit. On the other hand, perhaps American suspects are more violent and therefore any American cops who attempt to do the job without extreme muscles are unlikely to stay on the job. What do you think about this? What comes first, violence among criminals or violence among police officers? What can those who are lobbying for fairness towards blacks from their police force gain by reading your book?

Hoberman: The comparison between American policing and British policing is very instructive. There are about 55 million people in the UK, and their police kill about 25 people a year. There are about 320 million people in the United States, and our police kill more than a thousand people a year. The numbers from Scandinavia would no doubt be even more dramatic. Our policing style has become increasingly militarized since the 1980s. And, yes, many of the male cops you see on *Cops* do look strangely similar to each other. Police forces include many men I refer to in the book as "action-oriented." It is important to understand that this a masculine style issue that has serious consequences. For example, the vast majority of white police officers voted for Donald Trump, who has encouraged cops to treat their suspects more violently. In fact, Trump could not have been elected without the constant displays of his pseudo-masculinity and bravado. It is no accident that the motorcycle-riding crowd are his most loyal faction. Being or admiring Trump—like steroid use—promotes a "male" (read: aggressive or brutal) attitude.

Faktorovich: What advice do you have for new researchers who are interested in controversial topics, but are afraid that they might be criticized for venturing into these territories? Why is it important to discuss taboo topics? Why is it important for a researcher to write about the topics that happen to interest him or her at the moment rather than only the subject that is determining their future tenure?

Hoberman: Researchers interested in controversial topics should not be inhibited by the possibility—or, in some cases, the inevitability—of criticism and controversy. I can tell you from experience that the benefits of dealing with controversy greatly outweigh the initial emotional trauma. Doing good research that upsets people is an essential contribution to society.

Faktorovich: Thank you for chatting with me.

ALLEN M. HORNBLUM ON MEDICAL ETHICS AND SMEAR CAMPAIGNS IN SPORTS

Allen M. Hornblum is a Philadelphia based author who tackles controversial, historically under-covered topics in the areas of organized crime, Soviet espionage, and medical ethics. Prior to becoming an author, Hornblum had a varied career that included political organizing, college teaching, and many years in various facets of the criminal justice system. He has served in the Philadelphia Sheriff's Office, Philadelphia Prison System, and the Pennsylvania Crime Commission. Hornblum's research and books have been widely covered by the media and have been featured on Good Morning America, the CBS Evening News, CNN, the BBC, numerous radio shows, and just about every newspaper in the country including the front pages of the New York Times and the Philadelphia Inquirer. Hornblum is often asked to lecture on his research and has presented his work to a diverse group including; the National Institutes of Health, the British Medical Association, the FBI, numerous medical schools, as well as Brown, Columbia, and Penn State Universities.

American Colossus: Big Bill Tilden and the Creation of Modern Tennis: The indisputable force behind the emergence of professional tennis as a popular and lucrative sport, Bill Tilden's on-court accomplishments are nothing short of staggering. The first American-born player to win Wimbledon and a seven-time winner of the U.S. singles championship, he was the number 1 ranked player for ten straight years. He appeared in numerous comedies and dramas on both stage and screen and was a Renaissance man who wrote more than two dozen fiction and nonfiction books, including several successful tennis instructions books. But Tilden had a secret—one he didn't fully understand himself. After he left competitive tennis in the late 1940s, he faced a lurid  fall from grace when he was arrested after an incident involving an underage boy in his car. Tilden served seven months in prison and later attempted to explain his questionable behavior to the public, only to be ostracized from the tennis circuit. Despite his glorious career in tennis, his final years were much constrained and lived amid considerable public shunning. Tilden's athletic accomplishments remain, as he is arguably the best American player ever. *American Colossus* is a thorough account of his life, bringing a much-needed look back at one of the world's greatest athletes and a person whose story is as relevant as ever.

Faktorovich: Your books have been on topics that seem to have nothing in common, for example, organized crime, Soviet espionage, and medical ethics. How do you decide which topic you are going to focus on next? Have you considered choosing a single topic and zooming into it (as most academics or specialists do)? If not, why not? Your first two publications followed this more common pattern. First you wrote about human medical experiments in Holmesburg Prison (*Acres of Skin*), and then followed it with a book about a single African

American inmate who lived in this prison (*Sentenced to Science*). The press attention on the first study, must have inspired a second book contract from your publisher? Was the second book equally successful? Did you discover that you prefer to vary topics to make them more surprising or interesting for you to research?

Hornblum: It is true, my interests are quite eclectic. I'm certainly not your typical academic who focuses on one area of interest during his entire career. I'd find such a strategy quite boring though it might enhance one's academic career and authority on a subject. In addition to diverse interests, there are many interesting people, groups, and events that have been completely overlooked or in some cases forgotten. On many occasions when curious about someone—be it a gangster, spy, or athlete—its been disillusioning to discover that despite the person's significance nothing has been written about him. Many of these forgotten people or events are quite book worthy, but no one had taken the time to flesh out the story, do the hard historical digging, and write an accurate account of the individual or event.

That was the genesis of my first and probably most important book, *Acres of Skin*. When I first started working in the Philadelphia Prison System in 1971, I was stunned to see scores of prisoners strapped and wrapped in gauze pads and adhesive tape. Rather than a knife fight on the cellblock or a gang war in the exercise yard, the medical dressing was part of a vast and long running clinical trial program. In short, a prominent dermatologist and an Ivy League university had taken over the city jail and turned it into the nation's largest human research program testing everything from hair dyes and athletes foot medication to Phase I drug trials, dioxin experiments, and chemical warfare agents. Though it proved extremely difficult to acquire a publisher due to the controversial nature of the material, *Acres of Skin* on publication received a tremendous publicity around the world and is now considered a classic in the field of medical ethics.

Similarly, I've taken on research challenges regarding espionage agents and organized crime figures, and great but much forgotten sports figures. Granted, the investigation of little known historical figures demands considerable passion and time, but the satisfaction at the end of the process is all the greater. In other words, we already have 300 biographies of Ben Franklin, how about a good book about Harry Gold, a significant spy who gave the Soviets the secret of the Atomic

Bomb.

Faktorovich: Most of your previous books have explored crimes (corruption, medical malpractice), but your latest one avoids controversy and focuses instead on Bill Tilden's successes. You mention that there was a homosexual secret in his closet, but you do not look into the case that sent him to jail as you might have if you were writing about corruption in sports, or malpractice in Russian prisons. You seem to side with him, and you do not present too much evidence on the young man he was caught with. Why did you take this more scholarly, detached and less controversial approach with this book? Did you set out to make it hard-hitting, but discover that you sympathized with your subject?

Hornblum: I have to take argument with your opinion that Tilden is an uncontroversial figure. In fact, he was and remains sixty years after his death persona non grata in the eyes of many. Though unquestionably the Babe Ruth of tennis and one of the greats during the "Golden Age of Sports," he was also gay and late in his career found guilty of contributing to the delinquency of a minor. The convictions did much to dim his stardom and relegate him to the dustbin of history. Considering Tilden's impact on the sport of tennis as well as his other more cerebral gifts for writing, the theater, and music, it is amazing that so few people today know of him.

And I would have liked to pursue his criminal case and much speculated on sexual proclivities, but those avenues were closed off to me. Tilden's criminal files were lost by the LA County court system years ago and no one really knows or is able to document in any substantial way Tilden's sex life. Many of his closest friends thought he was asexual, and there are no documents or records of any kind illuminating his dalliances and romantic partners, if any. Now there are some journalists and biographers who would have a field day speculating about such matters, but I am not one of them. I base my studies and biographies on the evidence, not speculation. I have little interest in reading or writing fiction, hence I shall stick to the record, solid documentation, and what is provable.

Faktorovich: The reason you were chosen as an expert on the Holmesburg prison study is that you worked there as a literacy instructor for a decade and sat on the board of the Pennsylvania Prison Society during that stretch. You found proof of the experiments firsthand. You were a model employee during your tenure, being appointed to the board of the Philadelphia Board of Prison Trustees in 1986. You were hardly a silent participant, as you unsuccessfully lobbied to allow prisoners access to condoms. Why did you wait for a decade between your time at Holmesburg and writing about the abuses you saw there? The experiments went on between 1951 and 1974, and you say that you saw some prisoners who looked like they had wounds on their skin that seemed to be the results of dermatological experimentation while you were there, but did you arrive after the experiments had ended? Did you file complaints on behalf of inmates while you were employed there? Were you concerned about repercussions if you complained about the abuses while you were still employed at the prison?

Hornblum: From my earliest days in the prison system, I was convinced the medical research was problematic and there was probably quite a story behind such a large medical research operation in a city jail. Prisons, however, are not college campuses where information is shared and folks are encouraged to answer questions. In fact, they're paramilitary institutions and those who ask too many questions or start snooping around find themselves looking for a new job or worse. My initial inquiries were met with stock answers—the experiments had been going on for years with the blessing of the administration—and further advised to stop asking questions. Of paramount importance is that the entire city prison system had bought into a culture where medical research on prisoners was widely accepted and of long standing. No one to my vantage point raised concerns.

However, I knew something was amiss and expected that one day a medical ethicist, journalist, or historian would write the true story of what had occurred in the Philly Prison System. Years, in fact, decades went by without that book appearing. It was becoming increasingly clear that if I didn't write the book, if I didn't research the history of using prisoners as guinea pigs that unsavory aspect of American medical history would never be told. It would not be until the 1990's and while working in the Philadelphia Sheriff's Office that I began to track down former prisoners, search for doctors, and do a full court press for any documents that illuminated what had taken place in the city jail. After five years of intensive investigation—not to mention giving up my job to pursue the story more aggressively—did *Acres of Skin* appear on book shelves in 1998.

Faktorovich: Then you worked as the executive director of the Americans for Democratic Action, working on election and other political campaigns. A tie in to your writing on organized crime is your appointment to the Pennsylvania Crime Commission in 1988. Then, you were appointed the chief of staff of the Philadelphia Sheriff's Office. You eventually resigned from this role in 1994 to write the book on prison corruption. Did you intentionally take on these jobs within the establishment to understand how they worked so you could write about them, or did you feel the need to write about the topics you have covered because of your time in these roles (or both)? Why did you move into policing after all those years as a literacy instructor? Did you want the chief job so you could have more power to bring about positive change? What difficulties did you encounter in these attempts?

Hornblum: My career in the criminal justice begins in the early 1970s when I began working in the Philadelphia Prison System. Neither then nor for many years after did I have any interest in writing books. However, the close proximity I had to the clinical research program obviously impacted me and only two decades later did I begin to pursue the true story as to what had occurred. The experience of researching and writing *Acres of Skin* gave me an appreciation for books and the book writing process, which fostered the many books that followed. Already aware of various characters and stories that I thought were book worthy, I began to pursue subjects that I thought deserving of book length treatment. For example, Philly's Old Irish Mob and the Soviet spy Harry Gold were extremely interesting subjects who had been overlooked by authors. Their stories were compelling, but no one had ever taken the time or interest to flesh them out. Granted more work is involved in such research endeavors, but for those who like a challenge and the pursuit of interesting people, groups, and events, the extra labor is worth it.

Faktorovich: Given the current anti-Russian climate in America, your *Invisible Harry Gold* book about the life of an American spy in Soviet Russia, who turned and gave the secrets of the atomic weapon to the Soviets. Your Wikipedia page says that you "interviewed over 50 people" over the eight years you were writing and researching this project. What type of people did you interview for this project? Since the topic is spying, was it extremely difficult to get most of these subjects to talk (or did you avoid interviewing potential spies, focusing instead on more talkative subjects)? Why did Gold give the Soviets the information on the bomb? Did you research show that he was motivated by money, or was he threatened by the Soviets, or was there another reason? Was most of your research done in Russia or here in the US? What do you think about the current Russian election-hacking crisis? Do you think the Russians are guilty of this hack? What is the strongest evidence of this, if so? Could this recent hack also have been the work of a double-agent like Gold? While it's easy to see the benefit of an atomic weapon, it's difficult to understand why the Russians would want a corruptible, barely competent president. If there has been election fraud, isn't it more likely that the person who won the office and has seen financial gain to himself and his co-conspirators be a more likely fraudster than the Russians? Can the focus on the Russians be a diversion that builds on the innate American fear of Russians that has been brewing since WWII? Stepping back, what is your opinion on the tensions between Russia and America. Now that both of these countries are corrupted and capitalist, what is the philosophical disagreement that might be fueling renewed "hot peace"?

Hornblum: The individuals I tracked down and interviewed for the Harry Gold bio were mostly individuals who knew Harry such as doctors, neighbors, communists, FBI agents, etc. All described a sad, fascinating little man who had the best of intentions, but lost his way and began a long and secret service on behalf of Soviet espionage endeavors. Never motivated by money, Gold just wanted to help people, and was encouraged to assist the people of his parents' homeland—Russia and the Soviet Union. A sucker for a sob story and willing to give his last dime to someone in need, he refused to join the Communist Party but was willing to steal documents from his employer (industrial espionage) and ultimately, during the war, became involved in military espionage and what J. Edgar Hoover would refer to as "the crime of the century."

Faktorovich: You wrote an article for *Tablet* (a Jewish magazine), "How Black Prison Inmates in Philadelphia Were Turned into Human Guinea Pigs: A Memoir" (February 26, 2018). You compare the refusal of treatment to men with diseases such as syphilis in the Philadelphia prison system in the 1960s to the German's experimentation on Jews in the Holocaust, and yet, as you explain there were few repercussions for these American experimenters (while some Germans were executed for similar experiments). You explain how to-this-day, major companies are benefiting from the research that was performed in the 1960s on mostly unwilling or unknowing prison populations. Why do you think it has been possible for American experimenters to get away with this type of malpractice murder? Has the American public been brainwashed to believe that America is a hero of democracy and that it is incorruptible? For example, statistics show that few Americans believe their government is corrupt, whereas the numbers are higher in most other countries. Is there a difference between watching a prisoner slowly and painfully die of syphilis and the Nazis' experiments, and if so what is the difference between them? As you have continued writing about these types of inhumanities, have you noticed any shifts in public perception of these problems? If not, why not? Have you seen any policy changes as a result of any of your books or articles? If so, please describe the change.

Hornblum: The wide scale use of vulnerable populations for clinical trials during the 20th century is the underbelly of American medicine. Prisoners, developmentally disabled children, the indigent, asylum patients, and even newborn infants were all incorporated in ethically dubious research efforts. As I point out in *Against Their Will*, doctors knew where to go when they wanted to test a new elixir, a new treatment, or preventative treatments. Some of our most distinguished doctors and institutions bought into the practice, and all the while the general public paid little interest in this unsavory practice. The doctors who achieved fame and fortune though the test subjects—and there were thousands of them—are lost to history. Little more than human lab rats sacrificed on the altar of advancing science.

Regrettably, few Americans know of this sad chapter in American medical research. They remain convinced such practices only occurred in Nazi Germany. It is true, however, that while American jurists were putting the Nazi doctors on trial for their barbaric crimes, doctors in America were refusing to treat hundreds of syphilitic black sharecroppers, injecting hospital patients with plutonium, and infecting hundreds of Guatemalan soldiers, prisoners, and asylum patients with various sexually transmitted diseases. Not a record we should be proud of.

Faktorovich: Do you suspect Bill Tilden was set up by LAPD when he was stopped with the underage boy on the Sunset Boulevard? What was the reason the officer gave for pulling him over? Was his light broken? Was he speeding? Why would Tilden have let a stranger get behind the wheel of his car? Why would Tilden have kept his arm on the boy's lap in the time it took the officer to get out of his car approach his window? Does the story seem plausible to you? Did you find any proof as to the events of that night other than the officer's report? What is Tilden's version of events?

Hornblum: As to Tilden, he was obviously very deep in the closet as the times were not particularly supportive of gay men, even ones who held the status of celebrities. There is no reason to believe—at least at that initial arrest—that LA Police stalked Tilden in hopes of catching him with another man, but after that first arrest it is quite possible that Tilden merited special attention. The Hollywood community had garnered headlines for their extravagant lifestyle and rubbed some people the wrong way. Many in the criminal justice community targeted high-profile actors like Charlie Chaplin and Errol Flynn. Tilden was their equal in the international celebrity department and he no doubt came under greater scrutiny. That being said, there are many close observers who argue that if Tilden would have hired a more aggressive attorney, and utilized a more aggressive legal defense he would not have been convicted.

Faktorovich: Am I right in interpreting that you have doubts about Bill Tilden's homosexuality? You mention that he once said that he might have slipped into something related to the boy-incident when he was "young and stupid", and you describe Tilden as not "flamboyantly" homosexual. Did you find any proof that might suggest that Tilden had homosexual affairs as a youth or at any point later on? Were you surprised by the lack of such evidence (if you didn't find it)?

Hornblum: Though there is much speculation about Tilden's sexuality there is very little hard evidence of his associations. He was so bereft of obvious intimate companionship that some of his friends thought he was asexual. He had many friends—including kings and queens of

Europe and Asia as well as Hollywood royalty—but intimate, sexual liaisons cannot be substantiated. Arguably, those closest to him—his many gifted tennis students over the years—all swore that he was the model of decorum and never once showed or expressed any interest in them sexually. And I wasn't "surprised" by the lack of evidence after all these years, but I was definitely frustrated, especially so by the lost criminal records in Los Angeles County.

Faktorovich: What surprised you the most about how the game of tennis was played at its inception? Were there any shocking, corrupt, or otherwise tainted dealings you uncovered, or was it one of the more wholesome and untouched by scandal fields you have researched thus far?

Hornblum: If one studies the early years of lawn tennis, one can't help but be impressed by the class and cultural underpinnings of the game. Personal comportment, how one plays the game and carries himself, and the complete and total renouncement of professionalism and commercialism were the pillars the sport was founded on. Tennis more than any other sport was wedded to amateur play. Money and professionalism were vigorously fought against and this is the key reason there were no "open" matches between amateurs and professionals until 1968, which is very late when compared to other sports.

Faktorovich: Can you give us a brief review of the books Tilden wrote, especially his fictional compositions? Are you impressed with them? Do they show linguistic or structural mastery? Do you think publishers accepted them primarily because of Tilden's fame, or do they have literary merit?

Hornblum: Tilden was a keen observer and very accomplished writer. More than any other player of consequence, he wanted to foster the game. One of the ways he does this is through his articles and books. Many of his how-to tennis books like *Match Play and Spin of the Ball* are considered classics and still read by tennis players around the world. His fiction was geared to young people and tried to instill the values of hard work, loyalty, patriotism, and bravery in the face of opposition. As a child he had been much influenced by the stories of Frank Merriwell, and he hoped to accomplish the same two decades later by writing stories of young boys struggling to overcome obstacles in their lives. These tomes weren't meant to be great literature, but they were designed to teach young boys how to be men. As to his hundreds of newspaper articles, they are some of the most perceptive and visionary commentaries ever written on any sport.

Faktorovich: If a young person who is interested in writing journalism that gets to the heart of corruption in America is reading this interview, would you advise them to attempt to find work within the establishment they intend to write about? Why or why not? What advice would you give the young you if you met yourself when you were just out of high school? Should you have taken other roads? Was there a decision you wish you could change? Is there something you should have done earlier?

Hornblum: When I lecture at universities I tell students there are many stories still buried out there waiting for some intrepid soul to discover them. Corruption requires secrecy and the better the participants are at it, the longer the crime goes undiscovered. Some types of corruption are in plain sight and unfortunately becomes widely accepted. The Holmesburg Prison medical experiments are one example of just such activity as was the infamous Tuskegee Syphlis Study. But it's not just the medical arena that harbors such illicit practices. Government, higher education, sports all have their share of indiscretions just crying out for exposure. But the investigator has to be dedicated, able to do the heavy digging, and shrewd enough to connect the dots. Equally important, one has to be impervious to threats and the many obstacles that will be thrown in his or her way. It's not a vocation for the light of heart or the weekend warrior. Such challenges demand nerve, commitment, and a modicum of fearlessness that is all too rare today. But once the task is accomplished, one can take pride in a job well done.

Faktorovich: Thank you for participating in this interview. Would you like to comment on anything else?

Hornblum: Thank you for your interest in my books.

PROFESSOR MICHELE MCARDLE STEPHENS ON PEYOTE AND THE HUICHOL CULTURE

Michele McArdle Stephens is an assistant professor of Latin American history at West Virginia University specializing in Latin American communities. She previously taught as a visiting assistant professor at Denison University, and served as the Director of Latin American Studies at West Virginia University. She was a guest researcher in 2017 at the Max Planck Institute. She has a PhD from the University of Oklahoma.

In the Lands of Fire and Sun: Resistance and Accommodation in the Huichol Sierra, 1723–1930: The Huichols (or Wixárika) of western Mexico are among the most resilient and iconic indigenous groups in Mexico today. *In the Lands of Fire and Sun* examines the Huichol Indians as they have struggled to maintain their independence over two centuries. From the days of the Aztec Empire, the history of west-central Mesoamerica has been one of isolation and a fiercely independent spirit, and one group that maintained its autonomy into the days of Spanish colonization was the Huichol tribe. Rather than assimilating into the Hispanic fold, as did so many other indigenous peoples, the Huichols sustained their distinct identity even as the Spanish Crown sought to integrate them. In confronting first the Spanish colonial government, then the Mexican state, the Huichols displayed resilience and cunning as they selectively adapted their culture, land, and society to the challenges of multiple new eras.

By incorporating elements of archaeology, anthropology, cultural geography, and history, Michele McArdle Stephens fills the gaps in the historical documentation, teasing out the indigenous voices from travel accounts, Spanish legal sources, and European ethnographic reports. The result is a thorough examination of one of the most vibrant, visible societies in Latin America.

Faktorovich: You say in your "Acknowledgements" that *In the Lands of Fire and Sun* was a "labor of love" for you for "more than a decade. Did you start working on this project when you started your PhD studies? Did you develop your dissertation into your first major published book? Other than your general interest in the field, what inspired you to write about the Huichols of western Mexico?

Stephens: Well, originally I started studying Native American history at the University of Oklahoma and I had intended to write a dissertation on Cherokee and Seminole women. But I switched to Latin American history because, in the grand scheme of things, it is what I should have been studying all along. I did not choose to write about the Huichols, but instead, my professor who would eventually become my dissertation advisor suggested it as a seminar project in 2006. I wrote probably a 25-page paper on it, and then put it aside to focus on US history. But I was just not satisfied as a US historian, so after my comprehensive exams, I shifted to Latin American history and decided to write the dissertation on the Huichols. So, twelve years after that first seminar paper, the book is now a reality.

Faktorovich: In an earlier interview with the Max Planck-Institute you discussed how you feel safe conducting research in parts of Mexico: "Mérida, Yucatán is actually my favorite place to work in all of Mexico, because while it is a capital city, it never feels overwhelming in terms of size and population. It is very safe as well. Plus, on weekends I get to visit archaeological sites, which is important in helping to develop my cultural understanding of Mexico's past." You have traveled across the world not only for your research, but also to present at conferences in Oaxaca City and Mexico City (Mexico), Barcelona (Spain), Lima (Peru), and San Jose (Costa Rica). I lived for a year in Brownsville, Texas and visited Mexico for a single day, coming over the Arizona border in the previous year. There seemed to be a lot of tension under the surface when I was living or visiting these places. For example, a resort in Mexico pushed me aggressively to purchase something from their bar (I bought three closed cans), which in retrospect might have resulted in a drugging similar to the ones that have been plaguing tourists across Mexico. Why and how did you manage to feel safe in a capital city, where statistically the number of kidnappings and murders tends to be higher than in other regions? Are the places you go to, like the archeological sites, particularly safe? In other words, do you avoid going to resorts, restaurants, clubs and other places where drug or other criminal activity might be taking place? Are you careful to drive old, used cars or how do you check on your driver when you travel? Do you use public transportation? If a researcher is considering performing research work in Mexico, but the fear of potential violence or the like is stopping them, what advice do you have for them to practically avoid trouble, and to be safe on such an excursion?

Stephens: Well, things in Mexico are somewhat fluid at the moment, and crimes against women have increased in the last year or so. Nevertheless, Mérida is still really safe, so while I do have to go to other parts of the country like Mexico City, for the most part I take normal safety precautions as I would in any major city in North or South America. I do use public transit in Mexico City, as it's necessary to get to and from Mexico's National Archives (AGN) or the UNAM. If I am traveling alone at night, I will usually have my hotel call me a cab. Sometimes I will take an Uber.

Violence in Mexico tends to be higher where there are conflicts between rival drug cartels over territory. For now, Mexico City is not really contested territory, so there is not the same kind of drug-related violence as in other parts of the country, like Acapulco for example. Crime in Mexico City is like any other major city; in other words, it's random. So I am not going to be afraid to travel there, just like I would not be afraid to travel to Washington, DC or Paris or Lima.

I behave the same way in Mexico as I would in any other place, including my small town in West Virginia. I never accept drinks from strangers, nor do I walk home late at night alone. I don't wear lots of jewelry anyway, so that's usually not a problem. And if locals tell me to avoid a certain place, I listen to their advice.

That said, I have begun thinking of different ways to approach my research should the violence in Mexico become worse. The simple fact is that I am bound to restrictions by the US government, since I am a public employee and my research is funded by a state university or by government entities. Whether academics want to believe it or not, if violence increases to the point that the US State Department issues travel bans, there's not anything we can do about it. It's not paranoia to prepare for alternative scenarios; in fact, I just submitted a Fulbright application to do research in Mexico, and it required that I have a backup plan.

Faktorovich: Also in your "Acknowledgments", you thank several people for their help with your research. In my experience, archivists simply give researchers the folders they specifically request. Can you explain how you negotiate things with them or what kind of help you ask for to solicit the assistance you describe? You especially mention Fray Carlos in Mexico as a contact who assisted by "sharing books and documents" and you specify that Archivo General de Indias in Seville helped you analyze sixteenth-century documents because they were "outside of" your "comfort zone." Did Fray Carlos create a reading list for you of the relevant materials within your research realm? Did Archivo translate or decipher documents by lecturing you on their contents? You don't mention similar above-and-beyond assistance from the archivists at the Library of Congress and other places in the U.S. (where you also conducted archival research). Is it more difficult to solicit help from the U.S. archivists, and if so, why do you think this is the case?

Stephens: Fray Carlos at the Franciscan archive in Zapopan was a godsend to me as an historian. He knew his archive better than any other person, and knew what I would need simply by talking to me about my project. No other archivist has done anything remotely as helpful, or has given me more of their time than he did, either in the US, Mexico, or in Europe. In Seville, at the Archive of the Indies (AGI), the archivists were certainly sympathetic, as I am really not trained in Spanish paleography, so reading 16th century documents was not at all easy. But they were patient with my questions, and occasionally helped me confirm a word or sentence, and so that way I was able to determine whether or not a source was relevant to me. Then I had a friend help me make sense of the handwriting so I could figure out what I was reading.

In the US, archivists at the Library of Congress and at the Department of Anthropology archives in both DC and New York (at the Museum of Natural History, NYC) were as helpful as they could be; we must keep in mind that archives are often short-staffed, and employees wear many different hats, so looking after a graduate student or faculty member is not possible when they have so many other things to attend to. But regardless of where I worked, the archivists and other staff were always helpful with my occasionally silly questions, patient with my sometimes awkward Spanish when I was an early graduate student, and generally interested in my project.

Faktorovich: You describe that you have been "well-funded" by the West Virginia University, including a 2014 Senate Grant for Faculty Research, and the 2015 Riggle Summer Fellowship. You specify that most of the funding came in the final stages of your research. What did these grants cover? Did they cover your travels across Latin America, Europe and America to gather the materials from the archives? How important is funding to conduct advanced research (especially in your field)? Did some of the funds go towards paying archivists for digitizing, pulling or otherwise helping you process any of the relevant primary or secondary sources?

Stephens: The funding that I received from WVU allowed me to travel to archives in Mexico, Germany, and Spain in 2014, and Mexico in 2015, to finish researching and writing the first book. I conducted the research in the summers and I wrote during the academic year and sometimes in the summer as well.

I've received other funding from WVU to begin my new project, and have been awarded state-level (West Virginia Humanities Council) and international funding (Max Planck Institute for European Legal

History) for that work as well. All of the monies received goes to offset my travel and stays in Mexico or Europe. I process everything myself, mostly because I don't have any urge to turn that part over to an assistant. I am first and foremost a researcher and writer and I find it very uncomfortable to use assistants.

Faktorovich: You also thank "anonymous reviewers" at the University of Nebraska Press, and then name them (or perhaps the staff of UNP included in the second half of the sentence): Matt Bokovoy and Heather Stauffer. According to your CV, you have served as a manuscript reviewer yourself for the *Journal of Latin American Studies*, Rowman and Littlefield and the University of Nebraska Press. What is involved in the work of a manuscript reviewer? What kinds of criticisms or problems are the most common among those you offer on submissions? What advice do you have for researchers submitting their work based on your experience in these roles? Has serving as a reviewer helped you understand the perspective of publishers better, and thus increasing your chances of being published? Do you think having an established relationship with UNP helped you sell your book to them?

Stephens: Matt Bokovoy is the Senior Acquisitions Editor at the University of Nebraska Press and Heather Stauffer is the Associate Acquisitions Editor and both were instrumental in guiding me through the publication process. There were other folks who were helpful as well.

As for the reviewers, they remain anonymous, and probably will forever. To me, that is best. I've reviewed manuscripts and journal articles, and I find I can be honest and upfront with critiques; fortunately for me, the works I've reviewed have all been of excellent quality, which speaks to how strong the field of Latin American history is as a whole.

I am not sure I will ever understand academic publishing. Why some things get published and others rejected remains somewhat of a mystery to me. When I submit anything, I expect a lengthy process of revisions. It is pretty rare that materials are accepted for publication without revisions, at least in my experience. So patience is key here for anyone looking to obtain their first publication.

Faktorovich: In the "Prologue" you describe the story of Kauyaumari and his tribe and their struggles against an oppressor that forced them out of their homes, where they were near starvation until the gods, including Tamatsi Maxa Kwaxi saved them by giving them the "life-saving gift of peyote." You explain that the Huichols have used this founding myth as the center of their religious quest for peyote and worship of it. Peyote has been used by Native Americans across Mexico and what is now Texas for millennia before Spaniards invaded the region. The Huichol are one of the indigenous peoples who have utilized this hallucinogenic drug derived from a spineless cactus. You explain that this story is just one out of a rich cultural heritage of these people, which is connected to their ancestral lands, and that the invasion of these lands and attempts to push the Huichols out of them is equivalent to an attempt to wipe out this rich "cultural identity". Have you tried peyote across this research project, and if so, what was this experience like? Have you interacted with any living Huichol and if so, have you observed them consuming peyote, and if so what effect did it have on them? Why did you begin this book with the retelling of a myth about peyote without really defining what peyote is or discussing the legal or moral significance of the use of a hallucinogenic drug?

Stephens: No, I have not (and will not) take peyote, although I am asked this every time I discuss my research. This is not because of any objection to its use in general, but instead a profound disagreement with the practice of consuming something that is so sacred to another culture of which I am not a part. While there are plenty of "cultural tourism" practices that advertise the consumption of sacred plants or plant-derived products (peyote, ayahuasca), it is not something I have had an urge to do.

The Huichols are very suspicious of outsiders, as I think I make evident throughout the book. This is one of the first things I learned when I began researching this project in depth in 2008. It takes a very long time to "get in" to a community; this is the realm of anthropologists and sociologists I suppose, and for me, not the role I think historians ought to take if, as in my project, there is some historical distance. My book ends in 1930. I did not see a need to do fieldwork. Some disagreed with me on this point, and that's fine.

Lastly, I did not describe the legal or moral significance because there's no real need to do so. The story of Kauyaumari provides the context by which the Huichols have consumed peyote. It is the reason

I started the book with the origin story. And as for the legality, well, peyote occupied a liminal space in Spanish colonial society. In other words, while the Church frowned upon peyote use, indigenous use of the hallucinogen was never eradicated, nor was it made "illegal" in a way that we would understand it today. Spaniards prohibited its use by Spanish subjects, but the Huichols at least rarely felt the wrath of the Spanish judicial system for using peyote. In modern Mexico, it is technically illegal for anyone to consume peyote unless they are Huichol. But that has not always offered the Huichol protection, and I discuss an episode at the end of my book in which the Huichols faced some legal problems as a result.

Faktorovich: Texas does not allow for the drug use of peyote by non-natives even in Native American Church ceremonies. All U.S. states allow for non-drug uses in ceremonies by the Native American Church. In Mexico, peyote is only allowed in religious rituals. What is your opinion on the current debate over the legalization of marijuana? Are you for or against it? What about LSD or mushrooms? What separates the use of these hallucinogens from the ritual use of peyote by the Huichols? Should peyote be fully legalized alongside marijuana, or should it remain a Schedule 1 controlled substance outside of these religious uses?

Stephens: If I could solve the legalization question, I'd be rich. Or at the very least, I would probably have a different job. Personally, I think marijuana should be legalized and regulated like tobacco. This would certainly not solve the issues of cartel violence, as criminal organizations have already begun shifting their business to other illicit substances and activities. I don't support uncontrolled legalization of any other drugs, including LSD or hallucinogenic mushrooms. I certainly do not think peyote should be legalized for use outside of indigenous ritual. I've seen it sold as potted plants in markets in Barcelona. That was really strange.

Faktorovich: Where do you see the boundary between modern culture and ancient culture? For example, can a group of college students claim that they are following a cultural ritual if they annually meet to consume peyote or another hallucinogen? Would it become a cultural ritual if they invented a religion, or claimed that they were worshiping Huichols' religion?

Stephens: I take issue with so-called "cultural appropriation." It bothers me to see indigenous war bonnets on the heads of white people at the Coachella music festival, for example. This does NOT mean that non-indigenous people should avoid studying or learning about indigenous societies and cultures. But I have a fairly dim view of anyone who claims they want to commune with gods that they don't really understand, when what they really want is to get high. We see this a lot with ayahuasca ceremonies in South America. The Huichols do not use peyote for the high. I tried to make that pretty clear in my book. Their religious beliefs are incredibly complicated and I make no claims to understanding them all; but I've spent my professional career trying to figure out parts of their religious system, and I'd venture to say that random people who want to take peyote certainly don't understand Huichols or their religion.

Faktorovich: What would you say if somebody objected that the Huichols (instead of witnessing the death of their culture) were being assimilated into Mexico's government and culture when their settlements were attacked and they were forced to leave their lands or abandon their cultural practices?

Stephens: I think the world is closing in on the Huichols, as it is for many indigenous peoples around the world. But they've not assimilated yet nor have they lost their culture, and I certainly hope that never happens. In the 1890s, Carl Lumholtz, a Norwegian botanist who figured pretty heavily in parts of my book, believed that Mexican society was just about to overtake the Huichols. Well, it's 2018 and they are still a vigorous part of Mexican society that have managed to maintain their cultural identity. Being part of society while simultaneously distinct from it is possible and I think we see that in the Huichols of the 21st century.

Faktorovich: Why do you think peyote is disappearing from the Huichols' ancient trails: can it be that non-natives are collecting peyote to sell it in the illegal drug market?

Stephens: We're seeing it disappear I suppose because non-Huichols have no idea how to care for peyote. You can't just pull it up out of the ground; the Huichols know that the root system must remain intact so that more will grow. Destroy the root system and the plant is gone. I've heard of peyote being sold on the streets everywhere from Mexico, to the US, to obviously in Europe as I noted above. But I have no idea what the actual market is for peyote.

Faktorovich: You discuss the Huichols' annual return to the state of San Luis Potosi in Mexico, as a reclaiming of their "Holy Land". Their claims to this region have been confirmed through carbon dating of millennia-old ashes. You discuss how they did fight for their rights and became a Nation-State, before their started to lose territory and power across the nineteenth century. Can you clarify: have the Huichol people organized political movements to reclaim this region or a portion of it as their own reservation to maintain their ancient culture (as Native American groups have done with large-scale reservations in the U.S.)? Have they attempted to separate from Mexico into an independent state or country; are their numbers too low for this?

Stephens: There are no reservations in Mexico and the Mexican government's system of treating its indigenous populations has been different historically than that which occurred in the US. Not better or worse, just different. But what that means is that for the most part, there have been no attempts to form independent indigenous states in the 20th century. The Huichols did not form a Nation-State in their history. They simply have fought—successfully I might add—to maintain their ancestral homelands from exploitation. That does not mean that they haven't lost land—some Huichol towns were devastated by land laws in the 19th and early 20th centuries. But on the whole, they have kept their lands mostly intact.

Faktorovich: Can you recommend how the Huichols might fight to prevent future developments such as mining by the First Majestic Silver company or roads being built through sacred lands?

Stephens: I think they're doing a pretty good job currently. The Huichols work with outsiders when necessary, and their ability to partner with different NGOs has helped them ward off development in their lands in Jalisco (and in the west more generally) and in the peyote lands of San Luis Potosí. Mining is a significant threat, as is unchecked development in rural Mexico, and the rise of eco-tourism.

Faktorovich: Since you visited archives in Mexico, why didn't you take some pictures of the modern Huichol people for this book? You use a few great archival images of their art and photographs from a few decades ago.

Stephens: Well, I'm not an anthropologist, so I did not work in Huichol communities in Mexico. I like to keep a pretty significant historical distance from people or events that I study. I feel a bit awkward asking modern Huichols for their photograph when I am not writing about the present day.

Faktorovich: Are you connected to the Huichol culture personally? Are any of your relatives from this region? Do you identify with their beliefs? You discuss having a very large family in the front matter of the book, but mention that you have not seen most of them since 2000 as you have been busy building your career. Are the relatives you are referring to outside of the U.S.? Why haven't you been able to see them despite missing them? If not, other than a general curiosity about the history of native peoples, what interests you in the Huichol in particular?

Stephens: My entire family lives in the US and for the most part, in the northeast US. I moved to California shortly after graduating with my BA in History from Rutgers University, and have mostly lived away from New Jersey (where I was born and raised) ever since. I'm third generation Irish and Italian-American; my relatives came in the 1900s from Ireland and Italy. I am not Latin American or Latina or indigenous.

Faktorovich: You are currently working on your second book, *Women, Violence, and Legal Culture in Yucatán, Mexico, 1900-1930*. You mentioned in the interview response I quoted that Yucatán is one of your favorite places to visit. This state is on the opposite side of Mexico from the Huichols' ancestral lands. The Yucatán are on Mexico's tip on the Gulf Coast (near some of the major resort cities), while the Huichol live in the center of Mexico, a state away from its Pacific coast. The Yucatán has some of Mexico's major archeological finds, like the

Temple of Kukulcan. Other than both regions being culturally rich, they do not seem to have much in common and you have jumped from primarily studying the nineteenth century to the twentieth. Can you explain why you made this switch? What interests you about the Yucatán? The title of this book suggests that you will be studying crimes against women such as rape, sexual assault and the like; is this the case? Why is this topic a particularly significant subject to study regarding this particular region and time?

Stephens: There are elements of this new project that interest me a great deal personally and professionally. Being a historian is in some ways like being a detective. Working on historical crimes, against women in this particular instance, allows me to be a detective without actually having to engage with a deceased or abused victim, something I am not certain I could do. I much prefer working in the past than in the present.

Violence against women is a significant problem in much of the world, and Latin America is no exception. Femicides—or the murders of women simply because they are women—have skyrocketed in Mexico. The government there seems powerless to do anything about the increase in violent crime against women and girls. So this new study I'm working on can perhaps shed a little light on violence in the past. In other words, is the increase in crime today unique, or does it have some historical precedents in other periods?

The geographical shift in my work is based on two things: first, I like Yucatán. Mérida is smaller than Guadalajara and I am comfortable working there, because second, it's much safer than Jalisco. The state of Yucatán is the safest for women; Jalisco is somewhere in the middle.

Faktorovich: Do you have any advice for researchers who are just starting graduate school and hope to win research fellowships, become assistant professors and eventually publish books with top academic presses? What can they do to increase their chances of success in this tough academic market?

Stephens: My only advice is to be patient and open-minded. I was on the market for three years before I landed my job at WVU. That was in an academic climate that is far better than what we're seeing now. I also suggest that graduate students develop plans beyond becoming a professor. Learn how to market the very valuable skills that we have as historians. The ugly truth is very few PhDs get tenure-track jobs. I worked very hard, but was also incredibly lucky.

Faktorovich: Thanks for participating in this interview.

ESSAY

MIXED REALITY, THE FEMALE BODY, AND REPRESENTED WORLDS IN *WOMAN ON THE EDGE OF TIME* AND *SUCKER PUNCH*

Heather Duerre Humann

Abstract: The mingling of simulation with reality—oftentimes to the point that it is difficult to discern reality from fantasy or simulation—is a trend that has emerged in recent decades in both fiction and film. This practice of creating fictional worlds which mix science fiction with reality is symptomatic of a cultural disruption and also highlights 20th and 21st century cultural concerns, including contemporary anxieties about the female body. This essay addresses these concerns as they relate to two texts that are difficult to classify generically, Marge Piercy's novel, *Woman on the Edge of Time*, and Zack Snyder's film, *Sucker Punch*.

The mingling of simulation with reality—oftentimes to the point that it is difficult to discern reality from fantasy or simulation—is a trend that has emerged in recent decades in fiction and film. Bruce Sterling has labeled this emerging genre "slipstream fiction" (he coined this term, which he first used it in July, 1989 in an article that appeared in *SF Eye* #5). A short list of examples that demonstrate this trend include William Gibson's seminal cyberpunk novel, *Neuromancer* (1984), and Orson Scott Card's young adult novel, *Ender's Game* (1985), as well as a number of films from the 1990s and early 21st century, such as Kathryn Bigelow's *Strange Days* (1995), Alex Proyas' *Dark City* (1998), Josef Rusnak's *The Thirteenth Floor* (1999), David Lynch's *Mulholland Drive* (2001), Darren Aronofsky's *The Fountain* (2006), and Christopher Nolan's *Inception* (2010). This practice of creating fictional worlds which mix science fiction with reality is both symptomatic of a cultural disruption and, "an expression of our desire to situate and give shape to the moment," a point Veronica Hollinger and Joan Gordon argue in their edited collection, *Edging into the Future: Science Fiction and Contemporary Cultural Transformation* (3).

As Hollinger and Gordon suggest, the construction of these types of fictional worlds responds to cultural anxieties present in the late 20th and early 21st centuries, and this includes contemporary anxieties about the female body. The creation of these fictional worlds, however, raises new questions, as well, for, as N. Katherine Hayles and Nicholas Gessler point out, "when reality is mixed, ontological and epistemological issues tend to be foregrounded, because the represented worlds often cannot be assigned unambiguously either to science fiction or to ordinary reality" (483).Consequently, another important concern emerges throughout these works: the ontological status of the realities represented. This essay addresses these various concerns as they relate to two texts that are difficult to classify generically, Marge Piercy's 1976 novel, *Woman on the Edge of Time*, and Zack Snyder's 2011 film, *Sucker Punch*.

Both Piercy's novel and Snyder's film are noteworthy for the way they merge ontological questions with concerns about female agency, identity, and subjectivity. Although the film *Sucker Punch* was released thirty-five years after the publication of Piercy's novel, the two texts raise similar concerns and share much in common. Both texts feature female characters whose lives are largely defined by oppressive patriarchal societies and, in both cases, the women's suffering only increases after they are forced into mental institutions (in both cases, the women are wrongly institutionalized by abusive men). For these women, living in mental asylums means that they are not only denied their freedom, but they are also subjected to horrid abuse and unethical medical treatments. Indeed, their status as mental patients pushes them from already precarious positions of subordination to the point where they are nearly powerless. The only option for escape for these characters is to retreat to other realities, where they regain a degree of control over their lives.

Yet, in both *Woman on the Edge of Time* and *Sucker Punch*, the notion of escape is, in itself, presented as complicated, in large part because of the texts' use of "mixed reality." Since the represented worlds where these women reassert their agency cannot be assigned unequivocally either to science fiction or to ordinary reality, neither we (the book's readers and film's audience) nor the women themselves are ever fully sure what is real. Therefore, rather than their protagonists engaging with "reality" (singular), both *Woman on the Edge of Time* and *Sucker Punch* feature characters who must negotiate multiple realities.

Blurring Genre: *Woman on the Edge of Time*

When Marge Piercy's *Woman on the Edge of Time* was first published in 1976, many of the book's contemporary critics and reviewers did not discuss its genre at all, a point Margaret Atwood makes in her review of the book, which appeared in *The Nation* in 1976. There, Atwood laments, "none of the reviews of *Woman on the Edge of Time* I've read to date seems even to have acknowledged its genre" (Atwood 101). Atwood faults the reviewers who take Piercy's book to be a realistic novel and further suggests that the book, instead, should be read as a utopia—indeed, and as a number of scholars have noted, in *Woman on the Edge of Time*, Piercy uses the visitor-guide pattern, a common literary device in utopian writing. Though Piercy's novel clearly borrows elements from that genre, categorizing *Woman on the Edge of Time* as simply a utopia (or a dystopia, for that matter), neglects to addresses a fundamental issue: neither we nor the protagonists themselves are certain what is real. Indeed, even at the novel's conclusion, we are never fully sure what has really happened versus what has taken place inside the protagonist Connie Ramos' mind. In this sense, *Woman on the Edge of Time* functions as an example of "mixed reality."

A novel centering on thirty-seven-year-old Consuelo ("Connie") Ramos, a Chicana woman who is institutionalized following a confrontation with her niece Dolly's pimp, *Woman on the Edge of Time* details how, during her forced confinement, Connie communicates with an individual that may or may not be a product of her imagination—an androgynous young woman named Luciente who hails from the 22nd century. Really, it is never entirely clear whether Connie is merely hallucinating or if she is, in fact, somehow in contact with the future. Though Connie Ramos has been diagnosed as suffering from a violent schizoid personality disorder, she may actually be, as Tom Moylan argues in his book *Demand the Impossible: Science Fiction and the*

Utopian Imagination, "a sane woman labeled insane, a survivor reduced to a victim" (Moylan 123). For a while, Connie tries to convince the doctors that she has landed in the mental hospital by mistake, but because of how she is positioned socially, culturally, and economically—in other words, since she is a poor, uneducated Chicana woman—her objections to her diagnosis of insanity prove useless.

The individuals responsible for institutionalizing Connie are not merely guilty of misunderstanding her. Rather, Piercy depicts the lot of them—the pimp who has her committed, the institution's doctors and staff, and her own brother (who gives his consent to the experimental treatments the doctors want to practice on Connie)—as complicit in subjugating a powerless woman, a woman whose entire existence is governed by a system which seeks to exploit her. In fact, throughout *Woman on the Edge of Time*, Piercy takes pains to depict medical personnel, mental health professionals, and social welfare workers as not only sexist and condescending, but as part and parcel of the same patriarchal society that actively seeks to oppress Connie and women like her. Both inside and outside the asylum, Connie is silenced or ignored whenever she tries to assert herself. Even prior to her institutionalization, Connie has been personally subjected to a range of horrors, which Elaine Orr succinctly describes: "the scenes of her life include the physical violence of rape, coerced abortion, and unelected hysterectomy as well as the political equivalents: silence and invisibility" (Orr 62).

Once confined to the asylum, Connie Ramos faces more abuse and falls victim to unethical medical experimentation. Both inside and outside the asylum, Connie also observes the brutal abuse other women face, includes witnessing her niece Dolly being beaten and then forced into having an abortion and watching helplessly as other mental patients are neglected as well as physically and sexually abused by the institution's staff. The combination of what she experiences and witnesses teaches Connie difficult lessons about the limited roles available to her and women like her. Indeed, throughout her life, various forces conspire to keep Connie in a subordinated position, a point Elaine Tuttle Hanson emphasizes in her book, *Mother without Child: Contemporary Fiction and the Crisis of Motherhoo*d: "Taught by her ethnic and class background to be a good woman—a passive, submissive, complicitous victim—Connie is brutalized and abandoned by a series of men and institutions who are allegedly her protectors: her father, brother, lovers, husbands, professors, doctors, family, the welfare state, and the hospitals she is imprisoned in" (Hanson 160). Indeed, each time Connie comes into contact with members of the medical community or social welfare system, she ends up faring quite poorly by the interaction. Robbed of her daughter Angelina (by social workers) and her womb (via an unnecessary hysterectomy performed, Connie suspects, to give the doctors "practice"), then subjected to experimental brain surgeries ostensibly done to "cure her," Connie's existence as a marginalized member of society offers a scathing indictment of life under patriarchy.

Because of her subordinate position in American society, Connie, as Orr notes, "seems especially vulnerable to the experiments of her doctors" (Orr 65). Indeed, Connie is susceptible to violation on almost every level, for her "body can be entered from any direction by her cultural superiors—almost always men and frequently medically trained men"—and, this moving "into her body is coerced and violent") (Orr 65). A tragic irony of Connie's situation is that her status as not just a woman, but a mother—and her attempt to mother, that is, to fulfill the only role society permits for her—proves to be the catalyst for her confinement and medical maltreatment. As Orr points out, "both of Connie's instutionalizations stem from her mothering, the physical treatment she receives each time designed to cure her of voice" (64). With all the horrors Connie has experienced, it would be understandable if she were to create, in her own mind, an alternative reality to escape her miserable existence.

Indeed, one could interpret the novel in such a way as to suggest that this is precisely what happens to Connie. Others have argued, however, that Connie has, indeed, found a way to project herself into the future in order to visit the utopian society of Mattapoisett. Since Mattapoisett represents a sharp contrast to Connie's reality, it thus functions as an indictment of the racialized, genderized world that so oppresses her as a powerless and impoverished woman. Unlike Connie's own reality, Luciente is from a future free of pollution, gender oppression, homophobia, racism, class subordination, and consumerism. Contrasting Connie's institutionalized existence in an urban setting, the agrarian, communal community of Mattapoisett is populated by citizens who work together cooperatively and solve the majority of their problems via diplomacy and mediation. Connie learns, however, that life is not perfect in Mattapoisett, either; the death penalty continues to exist (no one wants to work as a prison guard, so repeat offenders are executed). Despite their Draconian punishment for repeat offenders, this reality nonetheless represents a stark improvement over Connie's world. As Ruth Levitas and Lucy Sargisson describe it, "Mattapoisett is as far from the poverty, neurosis, and alienation of Connie's present as is imaginable" (21).

The mere existence of a place like Mattapoisett serves as a critique of the social problems that afflict Connie in her realm. Mattapoisett's existence shows the possibility of a different type of world and, as Atwood points out, "if things can be imagined differently, they can be done differently" (103). While the contrast between the two realities highlights the problems plaguing Connie and her society, the reactions of Luciente and her peers to the problems Connie faces go even further toward indicting 20th century social, medical, and psychological practices. For example, at one point in the middle of the novel, Luciente notices that Connie is agitated and asks what is wrong. When Connie "described the ward and the project, Luciente grew still" (Piercy 216). It seems the more Luciente learns of Connie's world, the more pronounced her disapproval becomes. Despite Luciente's criticism of Connie's world, Connie is not altogether convinced that the changes represented by Mattapoisett are always for the best. For instance, in one of the novel's passages, Luciente describes for Connie how her society's technology has altered reproduction to the point that women no longer carry or birth their own offspring. Connie is confused to learn about this, so Luciente tries to explain:

> It was part of women's long evolution. When we were breaking all the old hierarchies. Finally there was that one thing we had to give up, too, the only power we ever had, in return for no more power for anyone. The original production: the power to give birth. Cause as long as we were biologically enchained, we'd never be equal. (Piercy 97)

Connie, however, is not persuaded that the method Luciente describes is better. She thinks of her own daughter ("Angelina, child of my sore and bleeding body") and ponders, "How could anyone know what being a mother means who has never carried a child nine months heavy under her heart…What could they know of motherhood?" (Piercy 98).

Further complicating this novel, there is a third level of reality introduced. Connie learns that Luciente's utopian society is only one potential outcome and that an alternate dystopian future is yet another possibility. Connie gets a brief look at that world and sees how generations of people practicing greed and oppressing others ultimately leads to dire consequences for much of that world's populace. In that reality, a wealthy elite live on space platforms and subdue the majority of the population with psychotropic drugs and surgical control of moods. They harvest the earth-bound humans' organs for their own use. The women there are valued solely for their appearance and sexuality; consequently, plastic surgery that gives women grotesquely exaggerated sexual features is commonplace. Yet, despite their vast dissimilarities, all three of these realities—Connie's world, the utopian future of Mattapoisett, and the dystopian future—are largely defined by their attitudes about the female body. Connie's reality shows the literal and metaphorical ways that 20th century patriarchy seeks to silence women and control their bodies—and this is particularly true for women like Connie whose lack of education, ethnicity, and social class leave them especially vulnerable. Mattapoisett shows the promise and potential of a society free of discrimination and gender oppression, but only presents women free from biological determinism once medical technology renders women's childbearing unnecessary. The alternate dystopian future shows by gross caricature the inevitable problems associated with treating women (and human beings in general) as objects and commodities.

Multiple Realities: *Sucker Punch*

Much like *Woman on the Edge* of Time, Snyder's 2011 film *Sucker Punch* raises provocative questions about female agency and subjectivity through the dilemmas its characters face. For much of the film, the audience is led to believe that *Sucker Punch* is about a young woman (known only as "Babydoll") who is institutionalized by her abusive stepfather and who then retreats to an alternative reality as a coping strategy. The film follows Babydoll as she devises an elaborate plan which will help her escape from the mental asylum. Much of the film's action follows Babydoll, who, "with the help of four fellow inmates, fights her way out through fantasy battle zones" (Dallas 54)[1]. Through Babydoll's narrative, the film presents an unflinching look at the precarious position of a young woman forced into a 1960s era mental asylum and awaiting a medically unnecessary procedure (a lobotomy), both of which result from her greedy and perverted stepfather's machinations.

As the film follows Babydoll's exploits, *Sucker Punch* forces the audience to consider whether the various realms that Babydoll escapes to—one represented by a high-roller's brothel and another depicted as assorted fantasy fight sequences—are the products of an abused and oppressed, but now disturbed, young woman's mind, or if they are, in fact, real. In other words, the film poses the question: Does Babdoll somehow travel to these imagined worlds, or are they, instead, landscapes she's created in her mind because she cannot cope with life in a mental institution? On the one hand, it would be understandable, given all the suffering and abuse Baby Doll's been made to endure, that her mind might create alternative realities where she could regain the agency that's been stripped from her. Yet, this interpretation is put to the test if we are to consider the significant degree of slippage between the various levels of reality represented.

Not only do Babydoll's adventures parallel the group's escape efforts, but what happens on one level of reality leads to very real consequences on the other levels of reality (for instance, during the last fantasy sequence, Rocket, another patient, sacrifices herself to save her sister, Sweet Pea, and is killed when a bomb detonates, which is paralleled by the cook fatally stabbing Rocket while she's trying to protect her sister). With scenes such as these, it should not be surprising that, like *Woman on the Edge of Time*, *Sucker Punch* has proven difficult to categorize generically. Dubbed "Alice in Wonderland…with machine guns" by Snyder himself, *Sucker Punch* is frequently referred to as an epic action

---

1   The adventures depicted include infiltrating a bunker protected by steampunk World War I German soldiers to gain a map (mirrored by Sweet Pea copying a map of the brothel/institution from Blue's office); storming an Orc-infested castle to cut two fire-producing crystals from the throat of a baby dragon (mirrored by Amber, another patient, stealing a lighter from the mayor's pocket); and boarding a train and combating mechanized guards to disarm a bomb (mirrored by Rocket, another young woman, and Babydoll stealing a kitchen knife from the cook's belt).

fantasy film[2]. These descriptions are somewhat informative, but they do not clearly address the question of whether the various sequences are real or imagined.

The audience is therefore often left guessing as to what is real versus what is happening in Babydoll's mind—and this continues for most of the film. It's because of the use of "mixed reality"—and the fact that the film's action and events occur on (at least) three levels of reality—that it is so difficult to discern what is going on in *Sucker Punch*. The film's conclusion, however, even further complicates these questions, because it interjects yet another possibility: that Babydoll, who we have long-taken to be the film's protagonist, is merely the avatar of another character, Sweet Pea, a young woman who is also trying to escape the asylum. The film concludes with Babydoll undergoing the lobotomy that her stepfather had arranged for her, while showing Sweet Pea fleeing the asylum for the promise of a better life.

In the following scene from the film, Babydoll seems resigned to her fate and even content with the fact that Sweet Pea will be the one to escape the asylum. Realizing that they are being pursued, the two women discuss their limited options:

Sweet Pea: This can't be. We did everything right.

Babydoll: A map, a fire, a knife, a key, one thing more, one thing more. It's me.
Sweet Pea: What?

Babydoll: [a breathy 'Oh'] Oh it's me, of course it's me. It's the only way this ever coulda been prevented.

Sweet Pea: What do you mean?

Babydoll: I'm saying you go home, go to your family. You tell your mom what Rocket 12 said, make her happy. Go out and live a normal life. Love, be free, you have to live for all of us now.

---

2   The description on the DVD case refers to the film as an "epic action fantasy," and reviewers, such as Sam Dallas who writes about the film for *Inside Film* review of *Sucker Punch*, have also discussed Snyder's characterization of the film.

Sweet Pea: Baby, no, you can't…

Babydoll: Yes Sweet Pea, you're the strongest. You're the only one of us who ever had a chance out there. You're going home and leaving, that's how we win. It's ok, it's better this way. Now listen, I'm gonna walk out there and when they come after me, you go, ok?

Sweet Pea: There's gotta be another way.

Babydoll: No, this is right. This was never my story, it's yours. Now don't screw it up ok? We then see Sweet Pea boarding a bus and starting her life anew.

What is particularly compelling about this exchange is Babydoll's pronouncement that, "This was never my story, it's yours," for this suggests the possibility that Sweet Pea is the author or creator of these imagined realms, rather than Babydoll. Ultimately, though, the film ends without fully resolving many of the provocative questions it raises.

The film's ending thereby comes across as rather ambivalent, leaving viewers left wondering about the ontological status of the worlds represented. Nonetheless, *Sucker Punch* succeeds in highlighting the oppressive nature of patriarchy, just as the novel *Woman on the Edge of Time* does. In yet another way like *Woman on the Edge of Time*, *Sucker Punch* shows the various forces that seek to define and confine women's bodies—indeed, this is true for all the levels of reality that the film presents[3]. In the 1960's era scenes, the female characters' lives are characterized by abuse (both inside and outside the asylum's walls) as well as literal and metaphorical imprisonment. Only further adding to this ambivalence, it is worth noting that there is spillover between the different realities in terms of characters. For example, a character who first presents himself only in a dream sequence reappears in the "real world" in the film's last scene. At a bus station, Sweet Pea is stopped by police as she tries to get on a bus to Fort Wayne, but she is rescued by

3   The film's brothel scenes show the hypersexualization and commodification of women, as well as the exploitative effects of such practices. The fantasy fight sequences allow the women a degree of agency and control, but this too remains problematic since these scenes show women forced to fight—sometimes to the death—to exercise such agency and autonomy.

the bus driver (the Wise Man), who misleads the police and allows her to board the bus.

Cultural Anxieties and Constructed Worlds

In *Sucker Punch*, a film that presents multiple realities and forces us to consider what is real versus what is imagined, just as in the novel *Woman on the Edge of Time*, we can see how the construction of fictional worlds responds to cultural anxieties present in the late 20th and early 21st centuries including anxieties about the female body. Ultimately, while both *Sucker Punch* and *Woman on the Edge of Time* raise more questions than they answer, they nonetheless succeed in highlighting the precarious situation of women under patriarchy, particularly for those women who exist on the margins, or who have been rendered voiceless by a system which seeks to oppress them.

Works Cited

Atwood, Margaret. *In Other Worlds: SF and the Human Imagination*. New York: Doubleday, 2011. Print.

Dallas, Sam. "Alice in Wonderland…With Machine Guns." *Inside Film* 139 (February/March, 2011): 54. Web.

Hanson, Elaine Tuttle. *Mother without Child: Contemporary Fiction and the Crisis of Motherhood*. Berkeley, CA: University of California Press, 1997. Print.

Hayles, N. Katherine and Nicholas Gessler. "The Slipstream of Mixed Reality: Unstable Ontologies and Semiotic Markers in *The Thirteenth Floor*, *Dark City*, and *Mulholland Drive*." *PMLA* 119.3 (May, 2004): 482-499. Print.

Hollinger, Veronica and Joan Gordon, eds. *Edging into the Future: Science Fiction and Contemporary Cultural Transformation*. Philadelphia: University of Pennsylvania Press, 2002. Print.

Levitas, Ruth and Lucy Sargisson. "Utopia in Dark Times: Optimism/Pessimism and Utopia/Dystopia." *Dark Horizons: Science Fiction and the Dystopian Imagination*. Ed. Raffaella Baccolini and Tom

Moylan. New York: Routledge, 2003. 13-28. Print.

Moylan, Tom. *Demand the Impossible: Science Fiction and the Utopian Imagination*. New York: Methuen, 1986. Print.

Orr, Elaine. "Mothering as Good Fiction: Instances from Marge Piercy's *Woman on the Edge of Time*." *The Journal of Narrative Technique* 23.2 (Spring, 1993): 61-79. Print.

Piercy, Marge. *Woman on the Edge of Time*. New York: Ballantine, 1976. Print.

Sucker Punch. Dir. Zack Snyder. Perf. Emily Browning, Vanessa Hudgens, and Abbie Cornish. Warner Brothers, 2011. DVD.

FILM REVIEWS

Samantha Lauer

*****

Coco: A Home-Run for Pixar

Within the Pixar universe, *Coco* stands on its own. It takes place close to present time, it's got twists and turns like a film for adults, and it features Mexican culture (a first for Disney) respectfully and artistically. From its songs to its voice actors and story, this film receives no complaint from me. Even in terms of the animation, Pixar demonstrates they can do new things, such as ghostly auras, glowing petals, and bridges between worlds. It's hard for me to give children's films five out of five stars, but I am pleased to be able to do so for *Coco*. It's definitely a story geared towards children, but it honestly provides a lot for adults to enjoy, and it even fights predictability in its script, characters, soundtrack, and plot. Sure, *Coco* taps into now-ubiquitous Disney themes (like fighting one's fate and following your passion despite your family), but this film somehow manages a freshness that Pixar hasn't been able to achieve since *Inside Out* (2015). In the end, I do give *Coco* five out of five stars for its ingenuity and its commitment to an evocative, stirring story.

Coco takes place in Mexico in the time of year around *Dia de los Muertos*, the Day of the Dead. As the film begins, rose petals, graves, and lit candles are our focus until the "camera" pans up. We hear music and see incense smoke rising from a censer, and a sense of ritual is established. The smoke rises through colorful sheets of paper forming banners that hang above the street, and the cut-outs of those papers tell the story we seek (see Figure 1). The banners reveal the history of the Rivera family, narrated by its youngest member, Miguel (Anthony Gonzalez). The Riveras are described as a close-knit group of shoemakers with a saddening past. Long ago, a couple of Rivera ancestors fell in love and had a child. The woman is Mamá Imelda (Alanna Ubach), while the daughter is Mamá Coco (Ana Ofelia Murguía), and the father is a huge mystery. After the father chose to pursue music rather than stay home with his wife and newborn, Mamá Imelda "didn't have time to cry over that walkaway musician." Instead, she formed a new life for herself and her daughter—a life that was wholly devoid of music.

Figure 1: To introduce this film, Miguel explains the story thus far, and it is demonstrated via animation through cut paper banners called *papel picado*. Mamá Imelda's fire (i.e.—dedication, will, ambition, and intent) is present from the very beginning.

Through time and the passing generations, Riveras continued to teach their children the evils of music. The Riveras became known by their business of shoemaking, and everything seemed agreeable until our protagonist Miguel (Anthony Gonzalez) came along. At the point where *Coco* picks up, Miguel is about 12 years old. He's still childish with frivolity, but he also has a sense of who he is beyond his family's music-restricted legacy. He narrates the introduction, "Sometimes I think I'm cursed because of something that happened before I was even born." This poor child *loves* music; all he wants to do is become a musician like famous local Ernesto de la Cruz (Benjamin Bratt), but he knows his hopes are limited, for he can't even mention his passions to his family without their harsh reproof. Miguel hides his talents as best he can until he can bear it no longer. On the eve of *Dia de los Muertos*, a talent show promises Miguel with an opportunity to play for others and receive feedback. Unfortunately, Miguel's family discovers his musical hideaway in the house, and they essentially ground him from music forever.

Figure 2: Miguel (voiced by Anthony Gonzalez) sits in his makeshift music room, watches Ernesto de la Cruz clips on repeat, and strums on his DIY-decorated, de-la-Cruz-inspired guitar. His dedication to his passions, despite all odds, is utterly stirring.

Miguel's rebellious nature as a character fits in perfectly to the mold formed by Pixar for its protagonists, and he can't be stopped by his family's traditions even if his Abuelita (Renée Victor) just broke his guitar and trashed all his musical equipment. Miguel knows what he wants and who he is, which is a musician through and through. He looks up at his family's *ofrenda* (the ritual altar set up for *Dia de los Muertos* that holds photos of deceased relatives, their favorite foods, and other offerings to their spirits), and he swears to Rivera matriarch Mamá Imelda that he will be a musician, but his friend, the street dog Dante, charges in to steal food from the *ofrenda* and coincidentally knocks down the photo of Mamá Imelda. This film suggests quickly, however, that there's no such thing as coincidence. As Miguel picks up the picture, he notices it's been folded to hide a pivotal clue in the identity of Imelda's "walkaway musician" lover: his guitar matches the one used by famous de la Cruz! Miguel connects the dots and rapidly assumes that de la Cruz must be his great-great-grandfather, so he charges to de la Cruz's grave to take the guitar he thinks belongs to him by blood so that he can play in the talent show after all.

Figure 3: Abuelita (voiced by Renée Victor), left, reminds Miguel (Gonzalez) of the *ofrenda*'s importance. The link this family has to their ancestors, which they validate each *Dia de los Muertos*, is touchingly beautiful. I commend Disney and Pixar for demonstrating this tradition so warmly and sincerely.

I thoroughly enjoy the way this film fights stereotypes and provides such a detailed and poignant depiction of Mexican culture. *Dia de los Muertos* is one of many Hispanic holidays that people from the United States capitalize on without fully understanding the context, but Pixar's work with *Coco* attempts to explain what's really going on without coming off forcefully or disrespectfully in its teachings. *Coco* demonstrates how real the world of spirits becomes on *Dia de los Muertos* for Hispanic people, and Mexicans in particular. I love the sheer beauty of this permeable worldview: The Land of the Dead overlays the Land of the Living in this film, and when Miguel tries to steal a guitar from the dead de la Cruz, things get wonky, and he's shifted over into the realm of the dead until he can get his family's blessing to return. The problem is that Mamá Imelda lives in the Land of the Dead, and she refuses to give Miguel her blessing unless he gives up music entirely. He doesn't try to force her decision, though. As an alternative, Miguel leaves his (dead) family's company to search for de la Cruz and receive his family's blessing through his father. On the way, Miguel meets Héctor, a lanky and rootless musician who claims connections to de la Cruz. Together, Héctor and Miguel travel to de la Cruz's home where he's hosting a huge *Dia de los Muertos* party for the dead. Here, things get interesting, and I refuse to spoil it for you. What I can spoil is that the supernatural realm is very real and very helpful in the world of *Coco*.

Figure 4: Miguel (Gonzalez) stands next to his loyal street-pup Dante and investigates the Land of the Dead in this shot. Its stacked style of housing is supposedly inspired by the way houses are built in various parts of Mexico.

Figure 5: Animal spirits called *alebrijes* live in the Land of the Dead as spirit guides, and the art for them is stunning. Eventually, even Miguel's animal guide Dante gets his own blessings, and enters honorary *alebrije* animation. In this still, renewed Dante attempts to fly over the back of Mamá Imelda's own *alebrije*.

Overall, this film succeeds in every aspect as a children's film, and it also exceeds my expectations. How Pixar still manages to produce films with songs that are as catchy as the classics from, say, *Toy Story*

(1995) or *Brave* (2012) absolutely blows my mind. I never thought I'd have songs from an animated film stuck in my head again; leave it to Disney to prove that I'm not quite as grown up as I thought. *Coco* also goes above and beyond what a children's film normally does with its plot twists. I'll just say that Miguel's assumptions about his family's paternity might not be all that accurate. Furthermore, the final scene between Mamá Coco and Miguel then solidifies that plot twist with one glorious, tear-jerking filmic moment. It's another Pixar home-run, without a doubt.

Coco's intricate visual humor follows with Pixar's past, too. For example, the technologies in the Land of the Dead are laughably appropriate since they're so outdated. Walkie-talkies, decade-old photo scanners, boxy computers, and filing cabinets filled with slips of information populate this literal and figurative Land of the Dead. I love that Frida Kahlo makes a cameo (in animation, of course), and her scenes are sure to be hilarious to both adult and child viewers who know who she was and what she stood for. The thought, time, and care put into this film is tangible. It actually sat on Pixar's workbench for 6 years during its creation, which is longer than any Pixar production schedule to date, but obviously all that time was well-spent because *Coco* is the new Pixar classic that this multicultural, globalized world needs. I recommend this film to virtually all viewers. If it doesn't warm your heart, I'm slightly concerned about you. I almost guarantee you'll love it.

Title: Coco
Directed / Written by: Lee Unkrich & Adrian Molina / Lee Unkrich, Jason Katz, etc.
Stars: Anthony Gonzalez (Miguel), Gael Garcia Bernal (Héctor), Benjamin Bratt (Ernesto de la Cruz), Renée Victor (Abuelita), Alanna Ubach (Mamá Imelda), Ana Ofelia Murguía (Mamá Coco)
Genre: Animation; Family Film; Comedy
Rating: PG
Running Time: 1 hr 45 min
Release: 2017

**

Mother!: If You Were Confused, It's Okay; Me, Too

I don't even know where to start with Darren Aronofsky's most recent controversy. *Mother!* tells the largely allegorical tale of a maidenly woman yearning to be a mother, however its complexities are multiple and nefarious. The film forces the viewer to question who this woman is, whether her desires are truly hers, what she's doing with this dude, and what is actually going on at all—but hardly any answers are provided. I've heard films described before by their trailers as "whirlwind adventures" or "rollercoasters" of one kind or another, and I honestly don't think I've ever experienced a truer depiction of those labels than with *Mother!* Reminiscent of *Rosemary's Baby* (1968), *Eraserhead* (1977), *The Conjuring* (2013), *The Shining* (1980), and other horror classics, *Mother!* addresses archetypally horrific themes one after the other, but that doesn't mean it's any good—or that it's even scary. Overall, *Mother!* seems to rely on a plethora of horror conventions rather than providing something substantive for the viewer, and I can't give it anything higher than two out of five stars for that, along with its failures in acting, plot, cinematography, and more.

Figure 1: In terms of camerawork and lighting, *Mother!* reuses the same scheme time and time again to depict the house as a shadowy force that engulfs each figure. This technique is effective but falls flat after a while, as do Aronofsky's dependencies on other techniques and plot pivots later in the film.

Figures 2 & 3: Two more examples of this high-contrast, setting-based lighting feature above.

While Figures 1 through 3 touch on the film's cinematography, it's time to dive into *Mother!*'s plot. As I begin describing this film, it will likely become easy to discern Aronofsky's attempts at allegory, for even the characters have no real names aside from their gendered associations or stereotypical roles. Here we go: *Mother!* features Jennifer Lawrence (Mother) alongside Javier Bardem (Him) as the quintessential couple. Him has been hurt (emotionally by something we don't know yet and physically due to the fire at his childhood home), but his relationship with Mother is promising. He's a writer and she's a homeworker. They stay in their big home in the middle of nowhere and hardly interact with anyone else until Man (Ed Harris) comes along and stirs things up. Mother is confused as to why Him lets Man stay, but his excuse remains that Man is terminally ill and wanted "to meet me [aka—Him, the great artist] before he's gone." This excuse becomes tiresome after a while.

Before long, despite the remoteness of Mother and Him's home, Man settles into his stay and somehow invites his wife, Woman (Michelle Pfeiffer), who shows up with baggage (of the physical, psychological, and emotional varieties) in tow. Mother spends most of this time fairly acquiescent and obedient to her husband and guests, despite internal and external stressors. When Man and Woman aren't driving Mother crazy, her anxiety still tends to spike because things get out of order anyway. As Mother loses her bearings more and more, the camera begins to shake, the visuals waver and distort, sound garbles, and Lawrence herself acts in great pain until her character runs to the bathroom to take a calming yellow powder dissolved in water. It's all very weird, and this context is just the start. Throughout Mother's interactions with Him, Man, and Woman, Mother also wanders the house with restoration in mind. She is the home-builder, after all. She finds herself in the basement where a crest in the wall starts to gather her attention.

Figure 4: Jennifer Lawrence (Mother) honestly does a great job acting as if there's an emotional connection between her and the house, although I'm not sure I understand why this connection is so important, given the ending of the film and the message I perceive Aronofsky to be expressing.

These four main actors all deliver performances that are focused but shallow, in my opinion, but the fault could be due to poor screenwriting rather than poor acting. Adding more actors to the mix just muddies the waters even further. Eventually, the sons of Man and Woman show up. Younger Brother (Brian Gleeson) arrives with Oldest Son (Domhnall Gleeson) right behind. There's bad blood between these half-brothers that escalates until Oldest Son kills Younger Brother on the floor of what will be Mother's child's nursery. Now the fun begins. Him, Man, and Woman run Younger Brother to the hospital and return with the news of his death. While they're gone, Mother cleans up the mess and tracks an annoying (and definitely supernatural) trickle of blood into the basement. It circles the seal she noticed earlier, which she bashes open to reveal an eerie tunnel full of gas cannisters. Mother doesn't stay downstairs long, though, because a huge crowd of people soon stream in to her house to mourn Younger Brother. They completely disturb Mother's serenity. Extremely intensified diegetic noise underscores the aggravating actions of incomers, and Mother's sanity unravels bit by bit until she explodes, banishing all the visitors from the house (for a time). It becomes clear by this point that the basically nonexistent soundtrack of the film attempts to embellish every frenzied moment with as little as possible. More than music, the film favors groans, sighs, clicks, and other innocuous or household sounds, and the technique is questionably effective.

Back to the story. With the temporary absence of these home invaders, Mother finally becomes pregnant, and her fertility inspires Him to write again. After he writes his book about her child, his "most beautiful gift," the word gets out and people start streaming into the house by the tens, fifties, and hundreds. The scenes that follow become a bonafide nightmare for the socially anxious among us. Him insists that the hectic presence of fans is simply because he's "trying to bring life into this house," so he never stops their coming, yet Mother's pain, frustration, and anxiety continue to increase. She insists that the child inside her is the "life" he could bring to the house, but all he can think of is his fame. She gives birth but can't trust him not to share the child with the hoard, and when she shuts her eye for a moment, that's exactly what he does. The child is passed around, brutalized, and killed by the crowd before they dismember and consume it in a twisted sort of communion. If you're thinking this movie shifted gears faster than a supercar, you'd be correct.

Figure 5: As things become more quickly and fiercely allegorical, more and more characters are introduced to the mix until we have this growing hoard in the end.

At this point in the film, none of the actions (of the main characters or the crowd) make any true sense, and the speed of everyone's actions increases exponentially, as if Aronofsky wanted to pack the most into this film but started running out of time at the end. Ultimately, the effect of the last third of the film is complete disorientation. Perplexity occurs with the characters, the plot, the setting, and more. All the while, images of the house from outside aerial view show the meadow around it burning inward. Sharing (to the point of abuse) takes center in *Mother!*'s scatterbrained plot. Kristin Wiig appears as Him's literary agent in her most darkly comedic role to date. Characters—with no name who are credited as Cupbearer, Philanderer, Fool, Damsel, Idler, Whisperer, and more—engage in devastation and destruction of Mother's house, child, and body with no respect, while Him seems utterly careless. At the close of the film, there's an explosion, a fire, and a grand reset. I'm not kidding! It's really out there, and you have to experience it for yourself.

When it comes down to it, *Mother!* really frustrates me because I can't figure it out. On the one hand, it's quite basic—frustratingly so. On the other hand, it feels like I'm missing something—like it's more complicated than I can grasp, but then I try to figure out what exactly I can't grasp, and I can't settle on just one thing. Overall, I think it's that

I just can't tap into Aronofsky's mission with this film. Either that, or I do kind of get it, but I'm not impressed with what I perceive. Darren Aronofsky titles the film "Mother," and he seemingly focuses on the track of women (and by extension, "Mother Earth") in society as culture and values have shifted, but he also puts much of his attention and glory, camerawise and scriptwise, on the male figure. The female lead becomes reduced to being only known as "the Inspiration" before it's all over. In the end, the female figure of Mother is literally replaced with a new female body entirely, but Him remains the same, with the same expectations of this new woman, as if to say that women come and go but the presence of patriarchy never changes, will never change its mission, and never varies in effect upon women of different types.

If Aronofsky's intent is to highlight the stresses provided to women (or "Mother Earth"), he's really missing something. Call it hope, intersectionality, independence, autonomy—call it whatever you will—but that's what this film lacks. Mother is the inspiration providing Him with the ultimate gift, which he then sacrifices to the masses willingly and presumably does it all again and again—either this is the most brilliant (albeit limited and hopeless) allegory to the recent treatment of women, or it's an intense oversimplification of systems that are already too commonly represented in film. At last, it comes down to my recommendation. I recommend *Mother!* to two main groups only: horror fans (please help me put my finger on why this film is so disturbing!) and Darren Aronofsky buffs (help me figure out what in the heck the director's doing here!). Others may want to just pass over this film when given the chance. It's a headache with static characters, inconsistent yet passionate actors, and a story you'll try to jump through hoops to understand. It's weird, it's scattered, it's pedantic, and it *claims* to be punk. Be wary and form your opinion yourself.

Title: Mother!
Directed / Written by: Darren Aronofsky
Stars: Jennifer Lawrence (Mother), Javier Bardem (Him), Ed Harris (Man), Michelle Pfeiffer (Woman), Domhnall Gleeson (Oldest Son), Brian Gleeson (Younger Brother)
Genre: Drama; Horror; Mystery
Rating: R
Running Time: 2 hr 1 min
Release: 2017

****

Annihilation: Sci-Fi Dabbles with Eco-Horror

Although Alex Garland's *Annihilation* didn't do as well at the box office as he and the crew hoped, this film has received mixed reviews from critics, and I firmly set my two cents in support of Garland's attempts. *Annihilation* demonstrates stellar visual effects, intricate plot points, moving acting performances, and intriguing narratology all while setting a new precedent for sci-fi as a genre and eco-horror as a way of using art to educate about the world. For some, however, *Annihilation* seems too scientific to follow, and others still argue it's complex and multifaceted yet lacking in substance. Furthermore, *Annihilation* didn't reach as many audiences as it could have due to its original and limited release through Netflix. Taking these accessibility issues into account, I give *Annihilation* four out of five stars for its message and artistry despite its limitations in relatability for various audience types. Overall, this film challenges the viewer to engage with their mind and its boundaries as well as their own responsibilities and restrictions in a dying world, and I absolutely adore it.

Natalie Portman (Lena) stars alongside Oscar Isaac (Kane) in this militaristic sci-fi adventure. Both worked in the United States Military together until Lena decided to pursue her academic career instead. Presumably, Lena and Kane ended up together before Lena became a teacher and biologist, but when her career changed, Kane still worked for the US Armed Forces. At the start of the film, Lena has accepted her first mission in years, but she's also been captured (or saved?) from that mission and is being questioned in a quarantine chamber about her journey. Right from the start, Garland works on building his world with the least details possible, and he demands you do almost all the work. For example, the viewer is cued into something strange at play with the fabric of Lena's reality as her captor asks how she ate over four months with only rations for two weeks or how long she thinks she was "inside."

Clues are provided along the way, but the heart of the adventure reveals itself in time. Garland's choices in editing refuse to allow the viewer too much context at once. He fragments the narrative in several interesting ways. First, there are three main sections of the story: "Area X," "The Shimmer," and "The Lighthouse." Then, each section delves into at least three essential timelines: Lena's experiences as a captive being interrogated in quarantine, Lena's memories of being with Kane when things were happy before he left for his own life-changing mission, and the mysterious timeline where Lena chooses to go "inside" for her mission after Kane returns. Once she's "inside," too, large swaths of time go unaccounted for, and the timeline gets even more twisted. On top of all that, the soundtrack of the film vacillates between two intriguing audio extremes, which disorient and invite the viewer. The first audio extreme demonstrates sci-fi-genre-typical ambient/electronic/industrial sounds, and the second exhibits gorgeous, slow, sonorous acoustic guitar. Each of these extremes is then punctuated by long-standing periods of intense and pointed silence. Ultimately, these storylines and musical textures intertwine and overlap like threads in a knitted blanket, and the ending reveals the intricacy of the overall design.

Figure 1: Eventually, we come to the main storyline, in which five professionals, scientists, and scholars (all of whom happen to be women) take on a tremendous, life-altering mission.

The eco-horror element of this sci-fi adventure has a brilliant message attached. It starts essentially thus: an alien lifeform has been colonizing a piece of Earth for years, and its effects on the landscape are equally unknown and feared. The original site for the start of colonization was a lighthouse on the Gulf Coast, and the US government has been observing its spread since the beginning. It's apparently easy to track the spread of what's called the Shimmer because of the way it looks. It appears like a giant bubble with rainbow sheen expanding over and engulfing the landscape (see Figure 4). What it's doing inside the bubble is rewriting DNA itself to splice every element of earthly existence together. As Josie (Tessa Thompson), one of Lena's team members, explains, "the Shimmer is a prism that refracts everything." This science-based explanation is where a lot of audiences become disengaged with the plot, for any number of valid reasons, but I find it completely fascinating. Inside the Shimmer, things get really interesting. The narrative becomes even more fragmented as Garland stretches time for his protagonists (a crew of all women who are experts in their fields) and plays with the very texture and content of reality with brilliant special effects. Garland and his crew re-envision every element of our world to produce scenes with trees that grow in the shapes of people (Figure 2), bears that roar with the screams of people they've killed (Figure 3), and air that ripples with rainbows like gasoline does in the sun (Figure 4).

Figure 2: These trees have apparently grown from the ground this way, under the influence of the Shimmer. At first glance, I assumed they'd grown from the bones of humans, but Garland's world is more intricate than that.

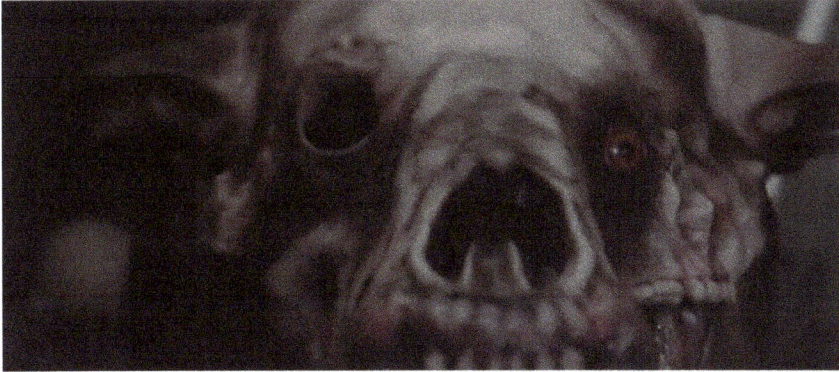

Figure 3: Here is the face of the bear whose roar captured the scream of its last victim. Note the human skull fused to the right side of its head.

Figure 4: Looking into the Shimmer from the outside, it looks like someone poured anti-gravity gasoline up into the air.

It's a strange world Garland establishes, and his eco-message is that the world seems threatened with something that can horrifically destroy it (the Shimmer), but, as Lena says in her quarantine interview, "It wasn't destroying. It was changing everything…making something new." Could it be that what seems like environmental devastation can become a new possibility by changing things up? Only the characters who go inside the Shimmer, though, are the ones who recognize this potential, so perhaps Garland also suggests that only those who are closest to environmental disasters will be the ones who know the best routes for change. What starts as eco-horror can actually be read as environmentally affirmative once the entirety of the message is unpacked. However, the plot can be understood multiple different ways, and some find the ending terrifying. If the ending is read as horror rather than thriller in its release, the message shifts slightly to imply something new entirely. It's all up to the viewer's interpretation, and I'm sure that's part of why *Annihilation* really divides audiences and critics.

Granted, *Annihilation* is kind of all over the place. Its plot, characters, settings, tones, and overall message are fragmented and up for interpretation. Its visuals are enlightening and transcendent at times, but they're also limited. Visually-shocking scenes occur only a handful of times, unfortunately, while the rest of the film seems like monotonous screen time in jungles, houses, and various other key settings. This film's characters are interesting but definitely underdeveloped and therefore flat. Its genre is kind of all over the place, too; is it thriller, adventure, mystery, psychological thriller, horror, sci-fi, or what? It could be that *Annihilation* is too many things and attempts too much to have an easy label, but that also means that people expecting any one of these genres will feel let-down by the film for its fluctuating nature.

Figure 5: *Annihilation* features the fragmented and shifting relationship between Natalie Portman (Lena), left, and Oscar Isaac (Kane). Their on-screen chemistry is appropriately tentative, powerfully emotive, and strangely relatable.

Finally, *Annihilation*'s overall concept is fabulous but highly condensed in this film setting, which isn't surprising because the idea originally comes from a trilogy of books written by James VanderMeer.

Garland's world-building is full of pride-worthy effort, but the ideas are clearly stretched too thin to have all the attention they deserve if he wants to develop any real depth. In comparison to Garland's previous and first film as a director, *Ex Machina* (2014), the built world of *Annihilation* leaves something to be desired, although the levels of care and energy extended for each film otherwise seem well-matched. In sum, the soundtrack astounds and the plot intrigues, but elements of *Annihilation* either leave audiences without a foothold or gloss too widely over concepts that had much greater possibility. I do recommend this film to all audiences, however. Give this film a chance. I'm also curious to see what interpretation you might have for this eerie psychological exploration of the worst our Earth (and our future) has to offer.

Title: Annihilation
Directed / Written by: Alex Garland / Alex Garland & Jeff VanderMeer
Stars: Natalie Portman (Lena), Oscar Isaac (Kane), Jennifer Jason Leigh (Dr. Ventress), Tessa Thompson (Josie), Gina Rodriguez (Anya), Tuva Novotny (Cass), Benedict Wong (Lomax)
Genre: Sci-Fi; Thriller; Adventure
Rating: R
Running Time: 1 hr 55 min
Release: 2018

***

Thor: Ragnarok: Another Generic, Listless Superhero Adventure

As one of about ten superhero films released in 2017, *Thor: Ragnarok* may be one of the best, but it still really isn't that great. This film is generic to a fault, and it avoids any substance of plot almost expertly. In place of true pith, the audience gets the same standard humor, costuming, effects, and characters as essentially all other superhero films, not to mention just the films with Thor in them. Perhaps the only interesting element of the film was the context of Norse mythology that's interspersed in the film, but even still, the characters and plot points dancing around that mythological backbone fall short of any sort of originality or freshness. Ultimately, I give this film three out of five stars, for its generic limitations are understandable, and they all do work together to create a somewhat enjoyable, albeit basic film. I may just be expecting too much of the genre, and I'm sure most audiences (especially superhero fans) would love *Thor: Ragnarok*, so it's for their sake that I settle at three instead of two or less stars.

Figures 1 & 2: Some interesting mythological backstory provided by the film details the fall of the Valkyries after they battled Hela for the fate of Asgard. In Figure 2, the Valkyrie we meet in the film, whose name is credited as nothing more than "Valkyrie" (Tessa Thompson), reveals memories of this event.

Thor: Ragnarok begins with a passing story that ends up being important in the end of the film. In matters of minutes, Thor (Chris Hemsworth) (who describes himself thus: "Basically, I'm a bit of a hero.") defeats and imprisons the fire god Surtur, whose role in mythology is instigating Ragnarok by causing the fall of Asgard. After Thor defeats Surtur in this scene, it seems like the fate that provides the title of the film (Ragnarok) gets immediately subverted, but things are obviously not that simple. As the story progresses through stylized fight scenes studded with Led Zeppelin themes, we learn that Thor has been missing for a while and that his devious brother Loki (Tom Hiddleston) has taken rule of Asgard in his place by pretending to be Odin (Anthony Hopkins), their father. But when Thor reveals Loki and his deceit, a void of rulership befalls Asgard, and a new player comes in to take the throne.

Figure 3: The depiction of Surtur disappoints me a bit. I know he's a fire god, but there's nothing special about him in this undoubtedly computer-generated image. In this scene from the end of the film, Surtur has been released from his prison, so to speak, and the team attempts to use his powers to overthrow their ultimate villain.

Apparently, Odin also had a daughter, Hela (Cate Blanchett), who was the first-born of his children. When Odin takes himself out of the royal equation, Hela arises from her reign over Hel (Norse version of "Hell") to claim ownership of Asgard, too. Thor and Loki try to fight her, but she is obviously stronger, and her control over time and space is, too. She breaks Thor's weapon Mjolnir, grows badass antlers, and follows her brothers as they attempt to escape through a portal. Just to make things especially interesting, she also separates them into different realms of time and space. Essentially, the rest of the plot revolves around Thor as he tries to find Loki and get back to Asgard to battle Hela again. On the way, a fellow Asgardian, Valkyrie (Tessa Thompson) finds Thor and offers him as a gladiator to Grandmaster (Jeff Goldblum), the ruler of a raunchy, prison planet called Sakaar. Here, Thor finds Hulk (Mark Ruffalo) deeply stuck in his green state, so the next segment of his mission involves talking Hulk into remembering that they're actually friends and co-workers (see *The Avengers* franchise).

By the time Thor gets Hulk to remember him and work with him, Valkyrie switches back to the side of the Asgardians, and Loki is discovered. All this happens just in time for the gang to reunite and head back to fight Hela, and when Thor *does* return to fight her with his crew, the script gives him hardly anything to work with. He goes on a weak diatribe but claims the ultimate reason Hela can't rule is because she's "just the *worst*." How…riveting. The whole plot trajectory feels desperately predictable, too, hinting at a complete lack of originality or, at least, lack of ability to surprise. Of course, the ending is then even more formulaic to the genre because Thor finds himself a lady love interest (Valkyrie) in the nick of time, and her loyalty to him ends up saving the day. Honestly, the whole romance subplot feels forced and out of place in the scheme of the rest of the film. I could have done without that segment entirely, and the film likely would have been better off without it, but of course viewers of today expect romance from almost every adventure film—to me, it's just another disappointing fallback.

Figure 4: Another disappointing moment in the film is the gladiator scene where Hemsworth (Thor), left, is forced to face his friend Mark Ruffalo (Hulk), who doesn't yet recognize him. Narratological tropes like this one occur as often as this type of comic-book-style special effects do.

What else disappoints about *Thor: Ragnarok*? Despite the new and little-known director, Taika Waititi, whose influence on the film could have been beneficial, I notice nothing special (although, that might be what the genre requires). The actors seem complacent to play incredibly stock roles, the script has nothing creative about it, and the excessive comic energy of the film makes it feel like a bad B film. I know *Thor: Ragnarok* comes out of the comic book universe, and this comic excessiveness (along with the inclusion of highly-stylized, effects-addled action scenes) may be a conscious move to incorporate more of that comic book vibe into the film, but it just makes everything feel cheesy and lazy to me. The plot, even (with its terrible transitions), could be amped up with less of the typical and more cleverness, but instead, viewers get Thor and his "I'm basically a hero" mantra, falling in love with another woman and fighting for his home again.

Figure 5: Ruffalo (Hulk), left, Hemsworth (Thor), Tessa Thompson (Valkyrie), and Tom Hiddleston (Loki) align and face Hela in the final battle. Every superhero film needs a moment like this, as we literally size up our cast just like the villain does. Things look good for our heroes this time; the sun shines behind them.

In my mind, *Thor: Ragnarok* demonstrates some of the worst that the Marvel universe has to offer. Its costuming is standard and already well-known, its script is lifeless and predictable, its special effects are far from original, its plot has no sparkle or complexity, and its level of originality can be easily described as "nonexistent." It's generic, formulaic, and absolutely lackluster. Still, millions of viewers love this film and ones like it. There's something about this wave of superhero films that leaves viewers expecting the next one and loving each new addition as soon as they're released. I suppose, from that perspective, *Thor: Ragnarok* is exciting because it combines Thor's story with Hulk's (Dr. Strange also makes an appearance or two!), and *Ragnarok* picks up from where both of their stories left off mysteriously in years prior. Furthermore, it gives Tessa Thompson another moment in the limelight, which she takes full advantage of as a supporting actress. Her success in this film and others in past years, like *Selma* (2014) and *Dear White People* (2014), likely secured her later role as Josie in 2018 with *Annihilation* (mentioned above). I'm hoping this work will propel Thompson into additional astounding roles in the future. When it comes down to it, *Ragnarok* isn't the most interesting, exciting, or creative film, and I clearly have my qualms with it, but I can admit it's a feel-good story for superhero fans. It's guaranteed to entertain most viewers, as a matter of fact. In that light, I recommend this film to essentially any audience. I'm curious to see if it's just superhero fans that love it, or if I'm right and there really is something missing at the heart of this film. Give it a watch, but don't expect too much from *Thor: Ragnarok*.

Title: Thor: Ragnarok
Directed / Written by: Taika Waititi / Eric Pearson, Craig Kyle, etc.
Stars: Chris Hemsworth (Thor), Tom Hiddleston (Loki), Cate Blanchett (Hela), Mark Ruffalo (Hulk/Bruce Banner), Tessa Thompson (Valkyrie)
Genre: Action; Adventure; Comedy
Rating: PG-13
Running Time: 2 hr 10 min
Release: 2017

TIMELESSNESS AND COMFORT: A PHOTOGRAPHY PROJECT

Fabrice Poussin

The America West is an amazing world of power and mystery. The geological history there is an incredible one. The purpose of these photographs is to remind the viewer of the awesome nature of our surroundings. After all millions of years are inscribed in every rock, break, crack and formation we do encounter on our many walks across the wilderness. Although the drama of the earth's force continues, it is not perceptible with the human eye as it would require to be sped up hundreds of thousands of time to see it as it occurs. The purpose of these images is to show the drama the natural world goes through on an ongoing basis. Full of color, shapes, sounds, odors as well as rugged surfaces to the touch, it stimulates all senses and brings to a deep, keen as well as intense sense of communion and communication.

CONTRIBUTORS

Heather Duerre Humann is the author of three books, Domestic Abuse in the Novels of African American Women: A Critical Study **(2014),** *Gender Bending Detective Fiction: A Critical Analysis of Selected Works* **(2017), and** *Another Me: The Doppelgänger in 21st Century Fiction, Television, and Film* (2018). She teaches in the Department of Language and Literature at Florida Gulf Coast University.

Samantha Lauer: A recent graduate of Bucknell University's Master's program in English Literature, Sam is currently afloat in the job market. Sam is a poet, critic, artist, and essayist whose work has appeared in *Muddy River Poetry Review, Sonder Midwest, Impossible Archetype, Witches & Pagans, Sage Woman*, and *Cinematic Codes Review* as well as on the website Taste of Cinema. Their scholarly interests include Literary & Film Criticism, Environmental Literature & Criticism, Feminist & Queer Studies, and Postmodern American Fiction & Poetry. Their general interests include not starving while retaining a passion for making art in this late Capitalist, Anthropocene world.

Fabrice Poussin teaches French and English at Shorter University. Author of novels and poetry, his work has appeared in *Kestrel, Symposium, The Chimes*, and dozens of other magazines. His photography has been published in *The Front Porch Review, the San Pedro River Review* as well as other publications.

www.ingramcontent.com/pod-product-compliance
Lightning Source LLC
Chambersburg PA
CBHW051701090426
42736CB00013B/2487